ABSOLUTELY
EFFORTLESS
PROSPERITY

Forthcoming Books By Bijan:

EFFORTLESS PROSPERITY BOOK II

The journey continues as Bijan shares the next thirty lessons that he received from Spirit. These lessons are designed to bring you to an even deeper level of experience and spiritual growth. But please don't rush the process! Take the time necessary to heal yourself, using Book I. You will know the time is right to begin Book II when you are at peace and feel prosperity flowing effortlessly in your life.

EFFORTLESS PROSPERITY FOR KIDS (Untitled)

Share this magnificent gift with your children. Each of the stories in the books described below not only supports and confirms the thirty lessons of *Effortless Prosperity* Books I and II, but also follows the same daily lesson in the same order. Now, the entire family can practice the lessons together. Your children will learn to connect with their inner guidance, experience total peace, and increase their sense of self-worth. As they recognize the miracles that occur daily in their lives, their behavior will improve and they will become more loving and joyous. Communication and understanding between you and your children will flow effortlessly.

EP for Children (Ages 2-7) - This book will capture the imagination of your toddler to seven year old. It is filled with lighthearted and loving stories that will delight your children and fill them with joy.

EP for Preteens (Ages 8-12) - Jason and Gabriel, two special brothers, will bring the stories and lessons of *Effortless Prosperity* to life through their adventures together.

EP for Teenagers (Ages13-18) - This wonderful book is full of interesting and funny stories that follow the thirty-day *Effortless Prosperity* program. In the most subtle way, it will introduce your teen to the hazards of alcohol and drug use, as well as negative and unhealthy associations. It is a ***must*** for every teenager.

101 MIRACLES OF EFFORTLESS PROSPERITY

This book is designed to bring you back into the light whenever you feel either uncomfortable or in turmoil of any kind. Open this book at random and you will get just the lesson that you need.

ABSOLUTELY
EFFORTLESS
PROSPERITY

BY

Bijan

Revised Edition

Effortless Prosperity Published by Effortless Prosperity, Inc.
P.O. Box 370703, Las Vegas, NV 89137-0703
(702)735-6559   Fax (702)731-9429
E-mail Address of Author: Bijan@anv.net

For Study Group Information or To Order
Call Toll-Free: 1-800-437-7750
or
www.effortlessprosperity.com

Printed in The United States of America

I dedicate this book to my mother, who was as wonderful in the physical life as she is now. Her ability to teach me and guide me is as profound and as effective today as it was before her transition into the spirit world. Her communication always helps . . . I just wish that she would stop the corny jokes! But, maybe it is her way of making sure I am listening to her.

ACKNOWLEDGEMENT

The inspiration for this book came to me from my guides who deserve all of the credit for its content. Their influence and words changed my life and have allowed me to share my experiences with others who are also being affected in extraordinary ways.

CONTENTS

TWO OR MORE PEOPLE WHO ARE
VIGILANT FOR THE LIGHT ARE MUCH
MORE POWERFUL THAN HUNDREDS OF
PEOPLE LIVING IN THE DARKNESS

To the many "angels" who have touched my life in so many ways with their unconditional love, support and encouragement, I give my deep love and gratitude. Though I have listed many of you for specific contributions you have made, I am also grateful for the many other ways in which you have helped to make Effortless Prosperity possible.

Thanks to Mirkalice who showed me the unlimited potential I have.

Thanks to Karen and Susan for the first edition.

Thanks to Cattel, Judith and Penny who kept me in the light.

Thanks to the first fifty students who put me in touch with the power of the Effortless Prosperity experience, and to all the students who came after and kept me there.

Thanks to Corey and Fran for their guidance, love and generosity.

Thanks to Mae, Ted, Mike and Jane for their office and computer expertise. Also Barb and Bob.

Thanks to Harriet and Justin for their revisions.

Thanks to Genece for her creativity.

Thanks to Timmy, Alana and Peter for their work on the radio program.

Thanks to Nellie and Ron for their unlimited time and energy.

Thanks to Kathleen and Les for typing.

Thanks to Susan for proofing and editing.

Thanks to Jan, Bill and Joyce for their skills in organization.

Thanks to Carrie and Shari for their corporation work.

Thanks to Norm, Doc, James and Stoney for their accounting.

Thanks to Lisa for her editing of the children's book.

Thanks to Joey and Dennis for promoting me nationally.

Thanks to Clarisa and Amir for always being there.

Thanks to my core group for their support: Ron, Ruta, Patricia, Dorothy, Stoney, Kathleen, Sandi, Susan, Rose, Mae, Corey, Fran, Samia and Harriet.

Thanks to Sandi who gave up the need to look good so that she could become magnificent.

My deepest gratitude to all the facilitators and volunteers who have given so much of themselves to help so many.

Thanks to my sister Terry and brother John whose unconditional love has inspired me from the beginning.

Thanks to my son Michael through whom I have learned many of life's lessons.

And finally, thank you Samia for your sweetness and growth. Your vigilance for the light is an inspiration.

HOW TO BE
EFFORTLESSLY PROSPEROUS

To be prosperous without effort, we must first decide to make peace our ultimate goal. To be in peace, we must know that our *only* function in life is to heal ourselves and others through our expressions of love and forgiveness. We do not have to get better jobs, second jobs, or work more hours. We do not need to add to our education, acquire additional degrees, make better contacts, or be around people who either lead us, follow us, or who are more successful. We need only to stay focused on our function of healing and our goal of peace as we participate in life through interaction with people in our relationships, jobs, and social activities.

One of the greatest benefits of studying *Effortless Prosperity* is that we become aware of how we project our own feelings of guilt and fear onto others. It is our ego that will always tell us we are guilty or afraid and that we do not deserve "effortless prosperity". Yet at the same time, ego will convince us that we need to get rid of our guilt—and we do this by projection. Once we understand this, we realize that everyone is our mirror. Whatever we see in others is what we have first seen inside ourselves. As we learn to see this as *our own* guilt being projected out and not *theirs*, we are able to forgive them. By loving and forgiving them, we are loving and forgiving ourselves and healing our own minds.

Every experience in life is an opportunity for us to do our function of healing. Though this may seem difficult at times, it is made easier when we practice and think about it as often as possible. *Effortless Prosperity* contains thirty easy and powerful lessons. These lessons have been prepared in such a manner that, when they are practiced, our egos are slowly pushed out of the way and Holy Spirit is allowed to enter. This provides us with all that we need to experience effortless prosperity. Also, these lessons have been designed to give us the vision to see that, through our ego-selves, we can do nothing. But with the help of Holy Spirit, our Higher Self, and our guides, we can achieve our ultimate goal of peace simply by doing our daily function of healing ourselves and others.

As we perform our function of healing, our lives will become peaceful and effortless. Everything around us will automatically fall into place and everything that we need will be provided for us (God knows what we need even before we ask). As long as we are vigilant for the light and we *always* choose peace, our life will be filled with effortless prosperity, effortless relationships, effortless health, and ultimately, effortless living.

HOW TO STUDY THIS BOOK

The *Effortless Prosperity* book is a guide into the realm of Truth, where we are divinely provided with everything we need to be totally prosperous. It has been created to produce maximum results in the shortest time possible. *Effortless Prosperity* is not a book to be read in one sitting, however. The total power and effectiveness of this course comes from the daily study of and vigilance for the lesson of the day. One by one, day by day, each lesson builds upon the next to create effortless prosperity consciousness. If you sincerely "live the lessons" 100% each day, sharing your miracles with everyone else or with an *Effortless Prosperity* study group, you will experience what it is to be effortlessly prosperous by the end of thirty days.

If you are not vigilant and are only partially committed to studying the lessons, you may need to practice them for more than one thirty-day period. It may take only one month to get it, or it may take six or more. Each additional month that you study *Effortless Prosperity*, however, you experience the lessons on a different level. Be patient and vigilant. It is easy to return to old habits and familiar belief systems. After all, we have lived with them for a long time. Change is most effective when it is gentle and gradual. That is why this book is made up of thirty simple—though profound—lessons that will help you create effortless prosperity.

As you study the lessons, you may experience some resistance. As a matter of fact, ego often raises three issues. At first, it will try to convince you that effortless prosperity is too good to be true. It will tell you that nothing is "effortless"—financial abundance, perfect relationships, and excellent health only come with hard work and long hours. Secondly, ego will try to reason that the miracles you experience are just coincidence. It does not want you to recognize Spirit and your vigilance for the light. Lastly, as ego begins to lose control, it will panic and may become desperate. On a subconscious level, you may feel that you do not deserve effortless prosperity. You may even experience guilt about the past or fear of the future. But this is just ego's attempt to distract you from all of the positive things that are happening to you. Remind yourself often that you are prosperous, joyous, and completely open to receive all of God's gifts. You deserve all that the Universe has to offer. If you remain steadfast to the Truth and trust God within you, you will see amazing results. Ego will place many obstacles in your way, all of which can be easily overcome. To each of these, simply smile and say to ego, "Thank you for sharing."

When beginning to read *Effortless Prosperity* for the

first time, start with the lesson that corresponds with that day of the month. For example, if you start on the 11th of June, read all of the lessons up to and including day 11. Then on the next day, read lesson 12, and so on.

It is recommended that you sit quietly for several minutes each morning after rising and each evening before retiring while you repeat your lesson for the day. Allow communication and spiritual guidance to come to you during this time. These lessons will put you in touch with knowing the truth of who you are, which is a child of God. Apply each lesson you have learned as often as possible throughout the day. As a reminder, you may want to write the lesson on the palm of your hand or on a piece of paper. Whenever you think of it, read the lesson to yourself slowly, with your mind's full attention.

Special Note: Since every lesson builds upon and confirms the previous lessons, some participants have found it extremely beneficial to reread each of the previous lessons along with their lesson of the day. As a result of bringing all of the lessons into their consciousness each day, they have experienced even faster growth.

HOW TO SHARE MIRACLES

Miracles are shifts in perception. They occur when we ask Spirit to help us to see something through Spirit's eyes rather than ego's.

Miracles are a natural occurrence; they are expressions of love. When they are not occurring, our flow of love is blocked and turmoil is the result.

Miracles heal feelings of fear, separation, guilt, and anger. They always fill everyone with peace, because when we share only the miracles, we are talking in the language of *light*.

By sharing miracles every day, we encourage ourselves and others to look for and remember them. The more miracles we look for, the more we will find.

It is recommended that you write your miracles in your journal as soon as possible, before you forget them. Given enough time, ego will try to dispel the miracles and make it difficult for you to remember them when it is time for you to share.

There is an important difference between telling a *story* and sharing a miracle. *Stories* include all of the guilt, blame, and fear leading up to the miracle, seeing the cause as being anywhere else but within ourselves. Ego likes to add to the story because it believes that the longer the story and the deeper the drama, the juicier the miracle will be in the end. However, the truth is that after several minutes of listening to someone share a story, our minds become so filled with the illusion of fear that we do not have enough capacity left to receive the miracle. We can literally feel the peaceful energy drain out of our bodies.

Stories always bring turmoil to both the speaker and listener. Limiting the shares (which are always confidential) to only two or three minutes helps to ensure against *story* telling.

HOW TO START AN EFFORTLESS PROSPERITY STUDY GROUP

The *Effortless Prosperity* study group is a thirty-day program that begins on the 1st day of each month and concludes on the 30th day with a potluck celebration. Each meeting starts with the joining of hands in a circle as the facilitator says a few words to bring the group together in spirit. This is followed by the reading of the day's lesson and assignment. The remainder of the one and a half-hour meeting is filled with the sharing of miracles. Donations may be taken in the final minutes. Before the meeting ends, there is a joining of hands as the facilitator says a few words in closing.

Effortless Prosperity study groups all over the world follow the procedure above. In addition, each one is doing the same lesson on the same day of the month. For example, if the study group were to start on the 11th day of the month, it would begin with the eleventh lesson. Likewise, if someone were to join a group for the first time on the 18th, he or she would start with the eighteenth lesson. By doing it this way, we are aligning with the collective consciousness of all of our brothers and sisters in the light, who are also studying *Effortless Prosperity*. There is tremendous power and effectiveness that comes forth when so many people around the world are doing the same lesson on the same day.

The global and personal benefits of *Effortless Prosperity* multiply greatly through the creation of daily study groups. The groups consist of two or more people who come together, at least once a day, to share the miracles they have experienced that day. The effect on participants is so powerful that eventually we begin to share miracles with everyone we meet and notice the light in everything we do. Miraculously, our lives are transformed. We see people differently. Our relationships either become joyful or end for our own best interest. We feel healthy and happy for no particular reason. And we experience financial abundance and prosperity. It is not unusual for some people to attend two or more meetings a day—especially when they are in turmoil. It is in these times of chaos (which always come from ego) when we most need to be brought back to peace and light. Once there, we can allow Spirit to handle everything else for us.

Participants who commit themselves for the entire month will see incredible results. The more vigilant they are for the light during those 30 days—by doing the lessons and attending at least one study group each day—the more overwhelming the benefits will be. Each time we participate in the group, our light is greatly extended. On the other hand, those who have not attended the group for a week often notice that their light is depleting, like a car running out of fuel. In order to increase the light, we must share it every day.

The *Effortless Prosperity* study group is a meeting place of peace, light, and love. It is not a therapy session, a 12-step program, or a religious meeting. It is a place where we share only miracles. We never preach or advise participants, and we do not network or discuss business. Darkness is never shared, nor are the long, drawn-out stories that often invite it.

The *Effortless Prosperity* study group is a wonderful place where people join together to share their shifts in perception and, by doing so, help the other participants to become aware of the miracles in their own lives. It is the one place where they can leave all of their problems outside the door and be enveloped in the light for at least ninety minutes each day!

INTRODUCTION

In the summer of 1995, after *A Course in Miracles* seminar, several people approached me. They said that they appreciated the sharing of my miracles because it helped them to make changes in their lives. They suggested that I write a book about them. I promised that I would think about it and ask my guide how he felt.

The next morning, after my meditation, I discussed the idea with my guide. He told me that I *was* going to write a book . . . but not yet. I responded, "Now would be a good time, since I am not very busy and it is fresh in my mind."

But again, he said, "Not yet."

I let it go. Around November, however, while in the middle of an intense workout in preparation for the Mr. Universe contest, my guide suddenly announced, "It is time."

"It's time for what?" I asked.

He said, "It is time for you to start writing the book."

I told him that I did not know what to write. He told me not to worry; he would handle it. He said, "I'll tell you what to say, and you write it down."

I began a long list of reasons why this was not a good time for me. "This would be the worst time," I insisted. " The real estate market is so busy and I am involved in several transactions. My diet requires a great deal of attention as I'm getting ready for this competition. And at this moment, I am involved in an intensive workout . . . I really don't have time to write a book."

He said, "I told you, it is time—you just do it."

Still, I had even more excuses for him, " . . . and as you know," I said, "I do not like to write and I do not like to read; I like to listen. My vocabulary, spelling, and grammar are not that good . . . so it's going to be very effortful."

And, again, he said, "I'll handle it."

Though I was very skeptical, I agreed and let it go.

That same afternoon, I went to my son's school to pick him up. While there, I ran into a friend who used to attend *A Course in Miracles* class that I taught on Monday nights. When she asked me how things were going, I smiled and told her what my guide had said.

"This is perfect timing," she said. She explained that her ex-husband usually did not see her children that often, so she was normally very busy taking care of them. But he had just informed her that he would like to have them two days a week. "Since I've written books before and am very good on the computer," she announced, "I would love to help you type your book." Suddenly, I realized what my guide meant when he said that it was going to be effortless.

For several months afterward, I drove to her home two days a week. After meditating with me, she would fix me a wonderful cup of tea and then type the miracles I dictated to her. Our thinking was in total alignment. This was necessary for me, in order to convey the message of the book. The level of mutual understanding, especially of my miracles, felt comfortable, natural, and most importantly, very effortless. Sometimes, it seemed as if she knew what I was going to say before I said it.

After several months, we felt that our work together was complete. I have a deep love for her and I am very grateful for her contribution.

When the book was finished, I found a printer with whom I felt I could easily work. After some discussion, we decided to print five thousand copies. But the very next morning, my guide told me to print only one hundred instead. This troubled me, since it was far more expensive to publish one hundred than five thousand. My guide assured me that I should do it this way, because I might want to add to the book . . . . Later, I found out that he was right.

One morning, during my meditation, I was enjoying an abundant feeling of thankfulness and gratitude for my prosperity. My guide appeared and explained to me that in order for me to be truly prosperous, I must share what I have.

Immediately, I responded, "Who do I give it to and how much?"

With a gentle smile he said, "In order for a person to be *truly* prosperous, he must share his *prosperity consciousness* with others."

I was puzzled, since I did not completely understand his statement. He continued by informing me that I was to hold study groups in which many people could learn about effortless prosperity. I was to select fifty people to participate in the first thirty-day "*Effortless Prosperity* seminar," where everyone could share their miracles and results.

I was skeptical and felt very uneasy about it. I reminded him that my English was not perfect and my vocabulary was limited. He told me that he would take care of it. I asked him, "How?"

"When you are addressing the people who come to your seminars," he replied, "just get yourself (your ego) out of the way *and I* will speak through you in such a way that those who need to hear the message I am sharing will receive it."

A warm feeling filled my heart as I realized that, with his help, I was going to be able to do this. Over two hundred and seventy people signed up for the first *Effortless Prosperity* seminar (but we had to choose only fifty). As time went on, I was guided and directed to specific people and places that would play a part in my offering additional *Effortless Prosperity* seminars. Everyone I approached gladly accommodated me and supported me on my path.

The most extraordinary thing was that all I had to do was show up at the designated time and my guide would provide all that was needed. To this day, whenever I think about an upcoming seminar, my ego panics because it thinks that I need to prepare myself. But then, I hear the reassuring voice of my guide telling me, "YOU NEED DO NOTHING."

I offer this book to you in hope that, by sharing my *"Effortless Prosperity"* consciousness, you will also experience the miracles that will help you to change your life with minimum effort and time. As your perception shifts, you will see your world differently. You will come to realize how powerful you are and that you are the creator of your own universe.

But this book is not about doing things, since *doing* is in the realm of effect and body. It is, however, about *being*, which is in the realm of cause and mind where free will and choice are possible. The results that you receive will be equal to the commitment you make to follow your daily lessons.

Bijan Anjomi,
Las Vegas, NV
March 1997

THE
LESSONS

Special Note: Whenever you feel unbalanced, become disturbed, or experience any kind of turmoil, reread the section in the front of the book, ***How To Be Effortlessly Prosperous,*** to bring you back to peace.

LESSON 1

I WATCH WHAT I SAY

This lesson is about being aware of all the things I say today. It is about looking at *what* I am saying, how much I am talking, and how much of what I am saying is making a difference in my life. Am I speaking for peace, or am I speaking for turmoil? Am I speaking to bring more love, or am I speaking to bring more fear? Throughout this day, I am aware of what I am saying and I choose only to speak words of peace and love to myself and others. *Today, I watch what I say.*

RECOMMENDED READING
You Always Get What You Want (p. 41)
Keeping Your Word (p. 43)

ASSIGNMENT FOR DAY 1
Be aware of how much you keep your word today.

LESSON 2

I NOTICE WHAT I HEAR TODAY

This lesson is like the previous one. It is about being aware of what really attracts me the most. Am I listening for miracles, peace, and love, or am I listening for stories, turmoil, and fear? I can make a choice to listen either to my Spirit or to my ego. At every moment today, I am aware of which one I am listening to and I refuse to listen to ego. *Today, I notice what I hear.*

RECOMMENDED READING
I Am Just the Messenger (p. 45)
A Message from "Our Friend" (p. 47)

ASSIGNMENT FOR DAY 2
Be aware of what you are listening to and whether you enjoy listening to your Spirit or your ego.

Remember to keep your word today.

LESSON 3

I AM AWARE OF WHAT I SEE

This lesson is about being aware of what I am looking at and what I am watching for. Am I more interested in looking at an accident and someone getting a ticket on the freeway, or do I enjoy seeing the sunlight filter through my window? Do I experience more powerful emotions watching someone fight than I do watching my child sleep? Am I interested in all the shooting and violence on the news, or do I look for people holding hands and expressing joy? When I realize that I have a choice of where and upon what I cast my gaze, I will choose to see the positive things. What I see affects my mind, and it is my mind that creates the world outside of me. *Today, I am aware of what I see.*

RECOMMENDED READING
Reliving Hurtful Experiences (p. 49)
Choosing Joy or Fear (p. 50)

ASSIGNMENT FOR DAY 3
Give some money away (not because the recipient deserves it). Bless it. Notice how you feel.

Remember to keep your word today.

11

LESSON 4

I DO NOT KNOW THE REAL
MEANING OF WHAT I SEE

Everything I see has a meaning that I have given to it. When I am willing to let go of thinking that I know its meaning, I notice that it is much different from what I thought it was. Today, I realize and understand that the meaning I give to anything has nothing to do with its real purpose. *I do not know the real meaning of what I see.*

RECOMMENDED READING
I Am Not a Body (p. 51)
Whatever You Resist Will Persist (p. 53)

ASSIGNMENT FOR DAY 4
Do something nice for yourself. Examples: get a massage; go out for dinner; treat yourself to ice cream.

Remember to keep your word today.

LESSON 5

I AM WILLING TO SEE THE LIGHT

This lesson is about being willing to see the light, which is always available to me. I allow it to come in and brighten up my day. I see it in even the darkest situations. Today I experience joy, love, happiness, prosperity, and abundance. I am open for miracles to happen. *Today, I am willing to see the light every hour of this day.*

RECOMMENDED READING
Recognizing a Savior (p. 54)
Uncovering the Light (p. 57)

ASSIGNMENT FOR DAY 5
Do something special for someone special.

Remember to keep your word today.

LESSON 6

I AM VIGILANT FOR THE LIGHT

This particular lesson is very powerful. It is about becoming more aware of my thoughts, and choosing thoughts of the light rather than of the darkness. Regardless of how attractive the thoughts of darkness look or how rewarding ego says they will be, I know the difference between light and dark thoughts. Today, I repeat the words "I am vigilant for the light" as many times as possible to myself. I choose light over darkness and love over fear. *Today, I am vigilant for the light all day long.*

RECOMMENDED READING
Going Home to Peace (p. 58)
The Game of Life (p. 61)

ASSIGNMENT FOR DAY 6
In the morning after reading the lesson, get quiet and ask yourself whom you have resentment towards. The first person that comes to mind is the right one. Make an attempt to contact him or her: talk in person; call on the telephone; write; or meditate and clear the resentment.

Remember to keep your word today.

LESSON 7

I AM VERY PROSPEROUS

What is meant by "I" in this lesson is not the ego and not the name that I was given at birth. It is who I really am, which is both God's extension and a creator that is undoubtedly very, very prosperous. If ego comes up today and tells me that I have no money in the bank, that I owe money to people, and that my job does not pay me enough, I simply remember that these things have nothing to do with who I really am. As an extension of God, I am very prosperous. The moment I believe this beyond a shadow of a doubt, everything around me will change to reflect this truth. My abundance is overwhelming and is waiting to be received by me. *I am very prosperous.*

RECOMMENDED READING
Prosperity (p. 63)
Expanding My Prosperity (p. 69)

ASSIGNMENT FOR DAY 7
When you get up in the morning, see yourself as a ball of light that is very powerful—like the sun. All day, walk around saying "I am the light."

Remember to keep your word today.

LESSON 8

EVERYONE WISHES TO CONTRIBUTE TO ME

This lesson is about realizing that everyone is making a contribution to my life. They want to help me with everything I do. They do not wish to contribute to me because of what I say or do; they wish to contribute to me because deep inside there is a knowing that I am prosperous, and at an even deeper level is a knowing that we are all prosperous. Their joy, their happiness, and their function is to contribute to me. I only need to receive and accept it as a natural part of my state of being prosperous. *Everyone wishes to contribute to me.*

RECOMMENDED READING
Weakening the Ego (p. 71)
How Prosperity Works (p. 72)

ASSIGNMENT FOR DAY 8
Give up control with one person (or one issue) for the day. Look at the result and your reaction to it. The result will be what is best for both of you.

Remember to keep your word today.

LESSON 9

I DESERVE PROSPERITY

This lesson is about knowing that because of who I am (a child of God), I deserve all of God's gifts. This is my inheritance. When I open my mind and heart, I allow prosperity to come forth to complete and fulfill me. And when I say "I deserve prosperity," meaning it from the bottom of my heart, I see myself as a very wonderful person who deserves everything that is good. *I deserve prosperity.*

RECOMMENDED READING
Miracles Are Not Sized (p. 73)
A Lesson in Forgiveness (p. 74)

ASSIGNMENT FOR DAY 9
Be dedicated to laugh. The more you laugh, the more prosperity comes to you. Laugh all day long. If people are with you, make them laugh too.

Remember to keep your word today.

LESSON 10

I AM OPEN TO RECEIVE
ALL OF GOD'S GIFTS

In this lesson, I literally walk around with my hands open to receive. I am not surprised when I realize that I am receiving without having to do anything. When someone offers to give me something, I accept graciously. I know that it is a gift from God. I enter into a feeling of thankfulness and gratitude inside myself. God hears my thankfulness and gratitude and responds with more gifts from many sources. *Today, I remember to keep saying to myself "I am open and receiving all of God's gifts."*

RECOMMENDED READING
Asking for What You Want (p. 76)
Remembering My Source (p. 78)

ASSIGNMENT FOR DAY 10
Walk around all day with your hands out to receive. Imagine your spiritual self walking around with hands out.

Remember to keep your word today.

LESSON 11

I GIVE AS I RECEIVE

This lesson is about knowing and understanding that giving and receiving are the same thing. It is just as joyous to give as it is to receive. It is just as joyous to receive as it is to give. When I receive joyously, the giver is healed by doing his or her function of making a contribution to me. When I give joyously, I am healed by doing my function of making a contribution to another. *Today, I give as I receive.*

RECOMMENDED READING
Forgiving Others to Forgive Myself (p. 79)
Cause and Effect (p. 83)

ASSIGNMENT FOR DAY 11
See at least one person as a child of God. Show this person unconditional love. You will feel honored to be in his or her presence.

Remember to keep your word today.

LESSON 12

I RELEASE ALL FEAR

This lesson is about letting go of my fear of anything and trusting God to take the fear away. The way that I let go is to know that fear does not exist. My fear is only my ego's deluded perception that it is possible to experience a lack of love in my life. To release this deluded perception, I must understand that I am always filled with and surrounded by unconditional love. Therefore, whenever I feel fear, I can bring forth this unconditional love and immediately the fear disappears. *Today, I release all fear.*

RECOMMENDED READING
Honesty (p. 84)
The Beauty of the Present (p. 86)

ASSIGNMENT FOR DAY 12
Write down five to ten prosperity affirmations. Repeat them throughout the day.

Remember to keep your word today.

LESSON 13

I OPEN MY MIND TO PEACE

This lesson is about opening my mind to the realization that there is always another way to view any experience in life. Whenever an experience does not bring me peace, I look at it from a different perspective. By being aware of the possibility that there is another way of looking at it, I create the opportunity for a peaceful resolution. *Today, I open my mind to peace.*

RECOMMENDED READING
Grateful Surrender (p. 87)
Excitement in the Present (p. 89)

ASSIGNMENT FOR DAY 13
Find a homeless person and give him or her some money. When you do, notice your judgment. That judgement is about you.

Remember to keep your word today.

LESSON 14

I RECOGNIZE MY OWN
BEST INTEREST

This lesson is about being aware that whatever I see is only a small part of the whole picture. Because I can not see the whole picture, usually what I think is good for me is not, and what I think will hurt me is actually helpful. I open myself to the knowledge that I do not need to take a chance on being right or wrong, because my own best interest is what is always being served in my life. *Today, I begin to recognize my own best interest.*

RECOMMENDED READING
Serving My Own Best Interest (p. 90)
Sharing the Lessons of Others (p. 92)

ASSIGNMENT FOR DAY 14
Hug someone that you normally would not hug. This is to be a sincere hug, not a quick one. What goes through your mind and how do you feel about yourself as you hug this person?

Remember to keep your word today.

LESSON 15

I AM PATIENT

This lesson is about being patient with myself and with everyone else. It is about knowing that time exists only to facilitate healing and growing. I see the difference between patience and procrastination. Today, I move effortlessly through my functions and activities with patience and love. *Today, I am patient.*

RECOMMENDED READING
Surrendering Control (p. 95)
Seeing the Truth About Myself
Through Others (p. 97)

ASSIGNMENT FOR DAY 15
Thank someone who you truly think deserves thanking. Come from your heart. How does it feel?

Remember to keep your word today.

LESSON 16

I PAUSE BEFORE I REACT

Because I know that my ego always jumps in first to respond to occurrences in my life, I need to pause and allow Spirit (love) to come through me before reacting to any situation. When I respond from Spirit, a result is produced that is beneficial to me and to everyone else. I pause, let go of my initial ego-oriented reaction, clear my mind, and ask for guidance. I receive guidance and act upon it. *Today, I pause before I react.*

RECOMMENDED READING
Love or Discipline (p. 99)
Judgment (p. 100)

ASSIGNMENT FOR DAY 16
Beginning today, start "being" instead of "doing." Expect a miracle—a BIG miracle.

Remember to keep your word today.

LESSON 17

I AM OPEN TO RECEIVE MIRACLES

Miracles are a natural part of my life and my acknowledgement of them makes them real for me. Miracles are the expression of Unconditional Love. They are always available to me; they are my inheritance from God. *Today, I am open to receive miracles.*

RECOMMENDED READING
Traffic Miracles (p. 101)
Remembering My Goal (p. 103)

ASSIGNMENT FOR DAY 17
Treat yourself special. Know that who you are inside deserves the best. Feel unconditionally loved. Give yourself anything that you want. Today, you are a king or a queen.

Remember to keep your word today.

LESSON 18

I CHOOSE ONLY PEACE

Today's lesson is about choosing peace over everything else. I choose peace all throughout the day. Every decision I make will be based on this. No matter what my options are, *today I choose only peace.*

RECOMMENDED READING
Gift from a Friend (p. 105)
Having Goals (p. 107)

ASSIGNMENT FOR DAY 18
Spend the day in silence. Do not talk to anyone unless you need to. Before speaking, pause and think "Will what I am about to say bring peace or turmoil?" Do not listen to anything today, unless you have to. If you must listen, notice how much of what you are hearing is coming from light and how much is coming from darkness. Today, notice how much of what you say or hear really makes a difference.

Remember to keep your word today.

LESSON 19

I AM A LOVING AND LOVABLE CHILD OF GOD

Today, I constantly repeat to myself that I am loving and lovable. I feel loving toward all others, and I am worthy of their love as well. I love myself, I love everyone, and everyone loves me. No matter what ego tries to tell me, I know that I am worthy of love. *Today, I know that I am a loving and lovable child of God.*

RECOMMENDED READING
Gifts from the Father (p. 108)
Projecting My Guilt (p. 109)

ASSIGNMENT FOR DAY 19
Continue to stay in peace. Repeatedly, say to yourself throughout the day: "Thank you, God", "I love God", and "God loves me".

Remember to keep your word today.

LESSON 20

ONLY LOVE EXISTS;
FEAR IS AN ILLUSION

Today's lesson is very simple. It is about knowing that only love really exists, and that fear is only an illusion. Fear is a lack of love, just as darkness is a lack of light. To remove fear, all that I need to do is bring forth love. I will then notice that the fear has gone and reality has returned. *Only love exists; fear is an illusion.*

RECOMMENDED READING
Love Does Not Punish (p. 111)
Seeing Through the Eyes of Love (p. 115)

ASSIGNMENT FOR DAY 20
Tell one person that you love him or her. Make it come from the heart. Notice the reaction. The person you tell will never forget that moment. Do it until you connect—until you really get it. Notice your reaction as well.

Remember to keep your word today.

LESSON 21

GOD LOVES ME
UNCONDITIONALLY

Today, I feel peaceful. I am so comfortable that I have a warm, fuzzy feeling inside. I know that God is taking care of me. The power of the Universe is with me and is protecting me from all harm. It protects me even from my own dark thoughts. As I allow all grievance, anger, fear, turmoil, and other negativity to fall away, my perception is changed and I am open to the unconditional love that is always available to me. *God loves me unconditionally.*

RECOMMENDED READING
Letting Go of What I Want (p. 117)
The Love of God (p. 119)

ASSIGNMENT FOR DAY 21
Hold someone's hand and tell that person that you love him or her unconditionally without speaking aloud. See the reaction—see if he or she gets it. Make sure that you get it.

Remember to keep your word today.

LESSON 22

GOD LOVES ME MORE
THAN I LOVE MYSELF

Today's lesson is about realizing that all of my experiences happen for a reason. I choose to see each one as a part of my personal growth. Because of this, I can give up control and let God lead the way. He knows what is best for me, far better than I do. *Today, I know that God loves me more than I love myself.*

RECOMMENDED READING
The Path of Life (p. 120)

ASSIGNMENT FOR DAY 22
Listen for God's voice to guide you. It will be most noticeable when you are making a decision. Be still and listen. God's voice always brings peace; ego's voice only brings turmoil.

Remember to keep your word today.

LESSON 23

I TRUST GOD

Today, I am aware that I have not been completely trusting God. When I trust God, I do not question any event that happens. I know that everything that occurs in my life is in my best interest. My power to create miracles for myself begins as I realize that I can make a conscious choice to trust God. *Today, I trust God.*

RECOMMENDED READING
Unfortunate Circumstances . . . or Gifts? (p. 123)

ASSIGNMENT FOR DAY 23
Listen for God within and embrace the peace He offers you. Then, notice and examine the experience that you have in your life because of it. Can you see the good (the silver lining)?

Remember to keep your word today.

LESSON 24

GOD IS GREAT, AND SO AM I

I already know that I am an extension of God. His quality and essence are within me. They are inherent and are my natural state. Because I am a child of God, I have the potential to be just like Him. God is great, and so am I. Whenever I need to bring love into my perception about someone, I close my eyes and repeat (several times), "God is great, and so are you." *God is great, and so am I.*

RECOMMENDED READING
Healing My Perceptions (p. 124)
Decision Making in the Present (p. 126)

ASSIGNMENT FOR DAY 24
Acknowledge how wonderful you are. Know that you are magnificent and you are growing toward the light. Know that many people are growing with you.

Remember to keep your word today.

LESSON 25

I LET GO AND LET GOD

Today, I get out of the way and allow the part of God that is expressing through me to come into my life and guide me. Today, I let peace make all of my decisions. I let love tell me where to go, whom to see, and what to say. I let the part of me that is God take over and make my life joyous. Today, I have the conviction that it takes to get out of the way and *"Let go and let God."*

RECOMMENDED READING
Looking Beyond Judgment (p. 127)

ASSIGNMENT FOR DAY 25
For one day, give full control to God. Do not take back the control. Notice how you feel being in His care and love all day long.

Remember to keep your word today.

LESSON 26

I AM BLESSED AS A CHILD OF GOD

This lesson is about knowing that, as a child of God, I have all of the gifts of life available to me at every moment. The gifts of love, joy, happiness, prosperity, abundance, peace, power, and choice are all mine. They are already in my life. As I acknowledge and recognize them, they continue to manifest more frequently and abundantly. My blessings are infinite, and I am surrounded by peace and effortless prosperity. *I am blessed as a child of God.*

RECOMMENDED READING
A Problem with Men (p. 130)

ASSIGNMENT FOR DAY 26
Bless people all day long (either silently or aloud). Say "God bless you" to everyone and mean it.

Remember to keep your word today.

LESSON 27

TODAY BELONGS TO GOD; IT IS MY GIFT TO HIM

This lesson is about giving and sharing all that I am. It is about totally giving up my control and dedicating everything to God. I know that today is already taken care of. *Today belongs to God; it is my gift to Him.*

RECOMMENDED READING
Our Function (p. 131)

ASSIGNMENT FOR DAY 27
Do not make any decision, small or large, without first asking God, your guides, or your angels. If the question comes from the heart and you are open to receive their guidance, you will get the answer.

Remember to keep your word today.

LESSON 28

I SEE ONLY GOD
IN ALL OF MY AFFAIRS

Today, I am completely vigilant for the light in everything I do. I know, at every moment, that everything happens to bring me closer to my goal, which is peace. Every action I take comes from my willingness to do my function of healing. *Today, I see only God in all of my affairs.*

RECOMMENDED READING
Where We Do God's Work (p. 133)
On the Death of a Loved One (p. 135)

ASSIGNMENT FOR DAY 28
Sit for fifteen minutes in a quiet place (later in the day is preferable). Look at yourself—at your growth. Acknowledge how far you have come.

Remember to keep your word today.

LESSON 29

THANK YOU, GOD

Today, I thank God for all that I am. Regardless of what my life looks like at this time, I know that every experience is occurring exactly the way that it is supposed to, for my highest good. I give thanks for it. I continue on to each new experience, knowing that it is better than the one before, because I now have a greater understanding of who I am. God is now in control of my life and I am very thankful. *Today, I thank God.*

RECOMMENDED READING
Healing (p. 139)
Guided by Spirit (p. 141)

ASSIGNMENT FOR DAY 29
Say "Thank you," (either silently or aloud) to all of the people you meet. Say it sincerely—from your heart. See them as God; see yourself as God. You are not thanking their egos, but thanking who they really are: the God within them.

Remember to keep your word today.

LESSON 30

I HEAR GOD'S VOICE ALL DAY

Today, I open my mind and heart in such a way that I can hear God speak to me and give me direction. I am open and able to receive His guidance. When He speaks to me, holy ideas come to my mind. God also speaks to me through my brothers and sisters when they are sharing their love with me. *Today, I hear God's voice all day.*

RECOMMENDED READING
If You Want to Know What You Want, Look at What You Have (p. 142)

ASSIGNMENT FOR DAY 30
Thank everyone for their inner goodness. Do not thank their ego. Thank the part of them that is God: their inner being.

Remember to keep your word today.

RECOMMENDED READING

YOU ALWAYS GET WHAT YOU WANT

Because I had not been on a trip for a while, I decided to take my eleven year-old son, Michael, on a short cruise to Mexico. The trip was planned so that we would be on the ship for New Year's Eve.

The morning before the day of my departure, I went to the gym to do my workout. I ran into an old friend that I had not seen for a while. I told him how excited I was about the cruise. He suggested that I would have a much better time being by myself and meeting other adults. Even though I did not agree with him, I noticed that the thought of being by myself on a large cruise ship excited me, and I began to wish that I were going alone.

After my workout, I picked up my son from his mom's house. He immediately informed me that he would not be going on the trip because he had no desire to be on a boat. After a few minutes of disappointment, I realized how fast my thoughts had materialized and that my wish to go alone had come true.

I drove to the hotel where I would be staying the night before my cruise. That evening, I had dinner by myself, then went to my room to relax and meditate. During my meditation, I told my guide that I would like to have my son on this cruise. He

41

told me that if I were sure about this, I should call him at his mom's house in Las Vegas.

When Michael picked up the phone, his voice was shaky. He was excited to hear from me. He told me how much he missed me and that he had made a mistake in his decision. I asked him if he would like to catch a plane and join me the very next day. Once again, I was surprised by how fast my thoughts were materializing and my wishes were coming true.

My time with Michael on the cruise was very joyous and I found myself truly happy to have him with me. We have to be open to see how fast our thoughts can materialize and our wishes can come true.

KEEPING YOUR WORD

I have a very dear friend who often tells me that the Universe is less than kind to him. Even though he makes a good amount of money, he always complains about scarcity and is never happy with what is going on in his life. His relationships usually fall through after a few weeks. Most importantly, he complains that he does not get what he asks for from the Universe. Many times he has asked me, "Why do you always get what you ask for?"

"I don't know," I'd reply.

Finally, I decided to consult my guide. My guide responded, "Imagine that your Father (your Higher Power, God, the Universe), is watching you with shimmering readiness and excitement, waiting to manifest your wishes. When you keep changing your mind and changing your word, saying one thing and then doing another, He gets very confused. Not knowing that His son can lie, He says, 'My son does not know what he wants. But since I am very patient, I will wait until he makes up his mind—no matter how long it takes.' Keeping your word is very important for your welfare," my guide continued. "If you give your word only when you are positive that you are going to live up to it, the Universe will come together to provide you with what you ask for. However, your friend is very confused: he constantly changes his mind after giving his word. As long as he continues to break it, the Universe will hold back."

"Shall I relay this information to him?" I asked.

"No, not now," he said. "I will let you know when to, since he is not yet ready for it." My guide then assured me that we are all growing along the right path. Though we do not have a choice as to the direction of our growth, we do have a choice of how fast we grow or how much we delay it.

I AM JUST THE MESSENGER

One morning, during my meditation, my mother (who has been one of my guides since her death several years before) appeared with another woman who was wearing a turban. I asked who her friend was. She replied, "This is Mrs. Bandar. She's the mother of your good friend, John Bandar." (He and I had been friends for nearly four years. John had come to America from Iran and is a reputable civil engineer in town.) I asked my mother what I could do for them. She replied that Mrs. Bandar would like me to give a message to her son. Knowing John as I did, I was not sure that this was a very good idea. But my mother strongly pointed out that I am just a messenger and should not make judgments. I agreed to give him the message. She told me to tell him that he should make a positive decision that day regarding a situation that he had been procrastinating about for the last two years. The decision had to be made that day. She emphasized that this message had to be given to John before noon.

After my meditation, I called John at his office. His secretary informed me that he was on the phone and had two other calls holding, so I left my name and number. Knowing how busy he usually was, I thought that it might be a day or two before he returned my call. Moments later, the phone rang— to my surprise, it was John. He explained that, for some unknown reason, the phone lines in his office had gone dead and had disconnected his other calls just seconds before he received my message. With an uneasy feeling, I relayed everything to him that my mother had told me. Laughing, he promised to enroll at the gym and work out with me. I told him that was not it . . . . He was quiet for about two minutes and asked me exactly what my mom had said. I explained it again, recalling her words to the best of my ability. His voice changed. He said, "Do you swear on your son's life that she said that?"

"Yes," I replied. He thanked me and hung up.

That evening, he called me at home and after some small talk, explained to me that for the past two years he had been given the opportunity to become a U.S. citizen; his mother's message had come on the last day of his eligibility. This surprised me—I thought he already was a citizen, since he had been here for so many years.

When I have the opportunity to pass on a message, my ego goes crazy and gives me many reasons why I should not. Whenever I get my ego out of the way and relay the message, however, I am always so very thankful for the results.

A MESSAGE FROM "OUR FRIEND"

In 1993, I began to receive a lot of messages from my guides for other people. I did not understand most of them, but acted as the messenger and passed them along anyway.

As I was meditating one morning, one of my guides, Moses, informed me that I was supposed to give a message to Tom. I asked him who Tom was. He reminded me that Tom was a gentleman I had met at the gym last week. I was a little uncomfortable giving him a message, since I did not know him very well. However, Moses assured me that it was going to be okay. Reluctantly, I asked him what the message was. He told me to inform Tom that what he had been waiting the last eight months for would happen that afternoon, and that he should not take any additional steps in regards to it. I agreed to pass it on, but reminded Moses that if Tom was not there, or if it was going to be effortful, I would decline.

A short time after my meditation, I went to the gym. I was pleased—but a little uneasy—to find Tom there. After some small talk, I told him that I had a message for him. He was surprised and asked me, "From whom?"

I replied, "From Moses."

He laughed and sarcastically asked, "You know Moses?" I explained to him that I meditate every morning and that Moses is one of my guides. He asked me what the "good ol' Moses" had to say. I repeated what Moses had told me. His face changed drastically: he lost his color—and, for a moment, I thought he was going to faint. He asked me to repeat the message again, so I did—exactly as it had been given to me. Then he asked, "Did he say anything else?" I said that he hadn't, shook his hand, and walked away. He picked up his towel and walked behind me . . . . He said that he did not feel like working out anymore, and left.

I saw him again about five days later. He ran up to me and gave me a warm, loving hug. He explained that he had followed the advice of Moses and everything had turned out perfectly. He thanked me and asked if I had any new messages for him. I replied, "No."

Over the next three years, I would see Tom once or twice a week, and just about every time, with a great smile, he would ask me if there had been any news from *our friend*. To this day, I do not know what the message meant to Tom, but I am glad that I was able to be of service to him.

RELIVING HURTFUL EXPERIENCES

When we get hurt, it would be easiest if we could let the pain go completely. But our egos want us to feel it over and over—ego's power comes from reliving the past—otherwise we would choose to release the memory totally. When we dive back into how or why it happened by describing and explaining the hurtful experience to others, we recreate and bring it forth to be felt again. Unless you want to relive the hurt, you must let it go.

CHOOSING JOY OR FEAR

Do you have joy and laughter in your life, or fear and anger? Do you like to watch happy movies and listen to people talk about their miracles . . . or are you drawn to fearful stories and disaster news? If you can look at these and see which you are attracted to, you will see what creates your world around you.

If you are attracted to fear and darkness, your world is about turmoil. If you are attracted to joy and light, your world is about peace. You can change your world by being conscious of what you are attracted to.

Walk away from darkness and fear; it isn't real anyway. Be vigilant for the light—this is your reality.

I AM NOT A BODY

Early in 1995, I was introduced to a very interesting book by Robert Monroe entitled "Journey to the Unknown." Shortly afterward, I read two of his other books: "Far Journey" and "Ultimate Journey." I consequently felt a strong desire to experience out-of-body travel myself.

I enrolled in The Robert Monroe Institute in Virginia for two sessions, back to back, each for one week. The atmosphere of the class was delightful and the trainers were more than kind and loving. I found myself enjoying the two weeks in Virginia tremendously. Along with some great friends, I experienced myself leaving my body on several different occasions. These experiences were exhilarating and very fascinating.

When I returned home, the thought of continuing the out-of-body experience was very much on my mind. So once again, I consulted my guide. He said, "Leaving your body and knowing that you can come back at any time is exciting, but it does not help you with your function, which is healing. You did not come here to leave your body. You came to heal your mind. If you need to leave your body, I'll take you and bring you back." Since that day, I have not intentionally left my body to accomplish a task.

The most powerful lesson I learned from both the Monroe sessions and the consultation with my guide was that *I am not a body.* My perception of what I really am was changed completely.

WHATEVER YOU RESIST
WILL PERSIST

Whatever you think of, you will bring forth. Whatever you choose, you will experience.

For example, if you are sad and resist crying, then crying will persist. If you are happy and you resist laughter, laughter will persist.

Whatever negative circumstances you accept, or become one with, will disappear.

For example, if you are in fear and say, "I'm not afraid—everything is fine." You will be *more* frightened, not less. The way to dispel the fear completely is to admit, "I'm scared . . . I'm *really* frightened!" You will soon begin to laugh.

If you do not resist what you are feeling and are willing to go through the experience, the feeling will lose its power over you, and you will be free to let it go . . . to create a new experience.

RECOGNIZING A SAVIOR

In 1983, I was living in Australia. For my vacation that year, I went to California to visit my family. Three days before my return to Australia, I attended a seminar with my best friend. Among the hundreds of people there, I noticed one particular woman. There was a tremendous energy between us. We sat next to her and later had breakfast together. As we were leaving the restaurant, my friend suggested that I give her a ride home. She and I spent the next three days together, effortlessly and joyfully—it was a very exciting time. There was intensity in the relationship that was remarkable. One month after returning to Australia, she joined me. Not long after this, she told me that she wanted to have my son. A few months later, Kathy and I were married . . . and in 1985, Michael was born.

When Michael was eight weeks old, we returned to the United States to live in Northern California. When he was six months old, we separated; Kathy moved to Las Vegas with Michael, and I moved to Southern California. In 1988, I also moved to Las Vegas because I wanted to be close to my son.

One day, when Michael was seven years old, I went to pick him up—but Kathy refused to let me have him. I could see that she was in turmoil, so I let it go.

After ten days of not seeing my son, my pain was tremendous. On several occasions, I wept uncontrollably—I really missed him. Still, Kathy would not answer my telephone calls.

At the suggestion of a friend who was a frustrated, divorced father, I attended a support group for fathers who were having difficulties with child custody. The anger in the meeting was almost overwhelming; I was astounded by the way in which these men referred to the mothers of their children. As I awaited a private consultation with the attorney who was offering advice, I realized that I was not where I wanted to be—or should be. I knew I had a very strong case (I had paid my child support regularly), but this was not about being right or wrong.

I went home to cry and to meditate, but my crying was so intense that I could not meditate. I decided to cry until I could cry no more. Finally, I felt the calmness in which I enter meditation. My guide came to me. I asked why I was being punished by such a horrible person. He offered a beautiful demonstration that became one of my most powerful miracles.

He asked me if I recognized who Kathy was. When I said that I did not, he said that he would show me. I was then surrounded by a circle of people . . . family, friend, and others whom I loved; some I recognized, some I did not. Then, my guide said to the crowd, "Bijan needs a savior . . . someone who is not afraid to risk looking horrible to him—this might be someone he will actually hate. Is there anyone who loves him enough to do this?" In the corner, someone volunteered. To my astonishment, when I looked, it was my ex-wife. She said that she would be steadfast in the game, until I got my lesson, regardless of how much I might hate her.

My tears began again. I knew that she was not my enemy at all, but rather my savior. Instead of anger, I felt love for her. When I ended my meditation, the entire house appeared different. For some unknown reason, I walked directly toward the telephone, and as I reached for it, it rang. I knew it was Kathy. She asked me how long I planned to keep my son waiting, because he wanted to see me. When I regained my composure, I told her that I would be right over.

This was an enormous relief for me. Of course, I was happy to see my son. But more evident was the absence of turmoil in my life. It was as if the weight had been completely lifted. Peace had returned. Since that time, I have never been separated from my son.

UNCOVERING THE LIGHT

When I was born into this world, I was a light. I was very happy, joyous, and totally delightful.

As time went by and my ego grew, it started to attract things. It stuck these things to me, then stuck other things to those things, and so on; ego likes to do that. These things could be anything from wrong thoughts and love of material possessions to fear, judgment, jealousy, anger, guilt and resentment. And as more and more of this stuck to me, less and less light came through, until eventually I could see almost no light at all.

I believe *A Course in Miracles*, *Effortless Prosperity* Seminars, and other quality thought systems that I have learned, have brought me in touch with how to remove this dark "stuff" surrounding my life. Now, my light shines brightly again.

GOING HOME TO PEACE

Shortly after completing the sessions at the Monroe Institute in 1995, I became very aware of my dreams. I would wake up every hour-and-a-half, after full dream cycles, and remember them vividly.

On one occasion the dream was so powerful that I could not go back to sleep. It started with my meeting a man named Tom while I was walking with my brother, John. Tom told us that he could take us to an alien world in an instant, assuring us that we could return at any moment we desired. But when he told us that our only function in that world would be to have a good time and be happy . . . we decided to go at *that* instant.

Almost immediately, we found ourselves in a magnificent green field that resembled a well-kept golf course. Warm sunshine fell upon the beautiful stream nearby and the fruit trees that were all around us. It was everything we had imagined heaven would be like. As we walked around, laughing and gorging ourselves on the delicious fruit, I noticed several people sitting down on the ground, aggressively guarding a few pieces of ordinary rock. I asked one of them what they were doing.

"As you noticed," he replied, "this planet is covered with grass. Rocks like these are very precious . . . .

To secure your future, you must have some of them underneath you."

Pointing at the fruit trees, I asked him, "With all of this food and water around, why do you want to hold on to those rocks?"

With a puzzled look, he replied, "Because there is more to life than eating, drinking, and being happy."

As we walked away bewildered, I noticed a small rock on the ground a few feet in front of us. Quickly, I picked it up and showed it to my brother, John. After examining it, we decided to look for more rocks. It wasn't long before we were sitting next to each other, guarding the few pieces that we had found. We didn't know why we were doing this, but even though it was effortful, it felt normal.

When I began to recount my rocks, a sense of fear and suspicion came over me as I realized that one of them was missing—I thought John had snatched it from me. I became enraged, and was just about ready to snatch it back from him, when Tom appeared.

"It didn't take you long to adapt to the ego of this planet," he said, smiling. "Have you forgotten that these rocks do not mean anything . . . ? Have you forgotten that you are here to laugh, be happy, and enjoy yourself?"

I told him that I wanted to return home because I did not feel peace here.

"When you are in peace, you are at home," he said. "If you want to go home, just *choose peace*. It does not matter what planet you are on. You choose peace or turmoil—heaven or hell—every moment. The decision is yours: your peaceful home, or your illusionary world."

Right at that moment, I woke up. From that night on, I have gone home more often than I ever did before. I haven't seen Tom since but I will never forget him.

THE GAME OF LIFE

In Las Vegas, gambling and gaming tables are a common sight to those who live here and those who visit. Imagine that life is played on two gaming tables: one is the table of Spirit, and the other is the table of ego. The chips that are won on Spirit's table are peace, satisfaction, joy, happiness, prosperity, abundance, integrity and love. On the other hand, the only chips that can be won on ego's table are hatred, fear, conflict, jealousy, anger, resentment, and grievances. The table that we choose to play on is— at every moment—up to us.

Once, a female friend of mine said to me, "Okay, I understand that I play on the table of Spirit, but my partner (my spouse) plays on the table of ego; and the only way that I can play with him is to go over to ego's table."

Well, my answer to that was, "Let him play as long as he wants to on the table of ego—he cannot play alone. And if you are strong enough, patient enough, loving enough—and do not leave the table of Spirit—sooner or later he will get up, walk over to *your* table, and start playing there."

As long as we continue to give love and refuse to allow ego to get involved, others will not have a choice but to come and play at our table. Once they play at Spirit's table, they can only walk away with the same things that we can walk away with: satisfaction, joy, happiness, etc.

And the wonderful thing is that at the table of Spirit, everyone always wins and no one ever loses. On the table of ego, however, everyone always loses and no one wins. If anything could be won on the ego's table, it would not be worth keeping.

PROSPERITY

I am one of four children from a very close family. Although we did not have many material things, we shared a lot of love.

I am especially close to my younger brother, John. Over the years, he has been a source of security to me, as I have been to him. We were always there to support each other in many ways, including financially. Whatever I had was available to him; he was my brother and there was a special bond between us. He told me, repeatedly, that I could rely on him for help of any kind, should I ever need it. I acknowledged this and knew it to be true. I believed that this privilege was one that I would never have to exercise, but its existence provided me with a feeling of security.

Ever since I arrived in the U.S. at age nineteen, I always had money, yet I did not recognize my financial wealth. Although I was a millionaire at one time, I never considered myself prosperous. My approach to prosperity was the traditional one: when I needed money, I would work harder. If my brother ever called for help with an investment, I was always able to accommodate him. Still, I never felt prosperous. The credit card companies apparently considered me to be a good risk because they extended credit lines of over forty thousand dollars.

I recall staring at the unused line of credit, thinking that maybe someday I should use it.

My security was short-lived, however. My income almost immediately evaporated as the bottom fell out of my business. Within six months, the thought of using the entire line of credit materialized. Although I was working hard in real estate, deals were not coming together; I went for several months without a successful closing. I was forced to take out a second mortgage on my home, and my car had a note. I had used my credit cards to live on, and they were "maxed-out."

I had less than one hundred dollars when, finally, it was time to play my "ace in the hole." I decided to call the one person who would help me without question or judgment: my brother, John. I delayed contacting him as long as possible, hoping that something would come through. I had trouble sleeping as I worried about both the money and when to call him; I knew that I had no alternative but to request his help.

I waited all day to make the call. He was very happy to hear from me, until I explained that I needed some money. His manner changed immediately—he became a businessman, not my generous and loving brother. He offered many excuses for why he could not give me the money. All the while, we both knew that he had it available. Although in the past I had loaned him as much as ninety thousand dollars at a time, he now thought that my request for five thousand dollars was excessive. Instead, he offered several hundred "for food." I explained that several hundred would barely meet my obligations and that I would not have asked if I did not need it. After I reminded him of the times I had assisted him, and after a lot of justification, he reluctantly agreed to send the money. I slept well that night, knowing that my brother was going to come through for me, just as I had known he would.

When I awoke the next morning, I noticed my telephone light blinking, telling me that I had a message. Although I was on my way to meditate, I decided to listen to it. It was my brother John, recorded at 2 a.m. His voice sounded strange, very down, and was lacking energy. He said, "Bijan-jon [Persian for 'beloved Bijan'], I have not slept all night. I have come to the conclusion that I can not help you. I have a family that I must think of first. I am very sorry."

I find it difficult to express how devastated I was . . . my brother had refused me when I needed his help. He was the one person I could rely on—I did not believe what I had heard. I replayed his message several times. I felt a total sense of panic, complete with chills and goosebumps. I was in shock. I sought solace in meditation, but I had difficulty letting go of my turmoil. I would wander around, get a drink, and then try again. After nearly a half-hour, I was able to meditate.

My guide came to my assistance. He said that I must be devastated. I told him that he was underestimating the situation. He asked if I wanted to be at peace. "Most certainly," I replied. He then asked me what my brother was to me. I answered, "My brother."

"No," he said, "you have made your brother a god. When you needed help, you turned to *him*, not your Father. Don't you understand that it takes much more effort to turn to your brother for help, rather than to God? God's gifts and God's help are available to you just for the asking, without effort on your part. The Father says that if we ask with conviction and faith, we shall always receive without effort."

I could not believe what I was hearing. "That easily?" I asked.

"Just that easily," he replied.

"Then, will I be okay?"—he told me that I was always okay—"Do I need to do anything?"—he assured me that I need do nothing.

Relieved and very peaceful, I moved to stop my

meditation. He asked me where I was going because my work was just beginning. I responded that he had just told me that I needed to do nothing. He continued by explaining to me the nature of prosperity. For me to learn this lesson, he, as my guide, had to take some things away from me. And, for the benefit of my lesson, my beloved brother John was in total turmoil. I was not to hesitate in healing and forgiving; I was to communicate with him immediately and extend my love.

With joy, I telephoned John. His voice reflected an exhausted being. He began by telling me that he did not know why he had done what he had to me. He said that he was willing to help total strangers, but could not understand why he'd ever hesitate to help the one who was so close to him. He was sincerely saddened, and offered his financial assistance in whatever amount.

I began to describe my miracle, not certain that he would understand. (His frame of reference was very different from mine.) He quietly listened as I outlined my lesson. I thanked him for his help in my growth and told him that I loved him.

Again, he offered his financial help. I explained that he had already helped me so much; everything was okay and I would not need his financial support. To my surprise and delight (and relief), he said that he understood.

Within days, the most unlikely real estate deals began to close. Within weeks, my credit cards were completely paid off. Within a few months, my car note and second mortgage were paid in full. Without effort on my part, but with complete enjoyment, deals were closing quickly and easily.

Since that time, my relationship with my brother has become even stronger. I love him fully as my brother, not as a god. I am greatly privileged to have him in my life. To this day, I am a very prosperous person.

EXPANDING MY PROSPERITY

One day, I received a call from an Arabian gentleman named Mustafah who was interested in having me weight-train his son. After a couple of meetings, he asked me if I would work on some property deals. Being a prince of Arabia, he had plenty of money coming to him. I gladly agreed.

Before I knew it, I had several big deals in escrow. Some of the commissions were more than I had ever dreamed of making, and the work was effortless. This continued for many months but the story was always the same: no closings!

One day, Mustafah told me that because of the exchange of currency and the delay of his funds, he was in need of some quick cash. I offered him what I had in the bank, which was three thousand dollars. He graciously accepted and promised that he would pay it off within a few days. Unfortunately, he did not. And after a year of his escrows falling through, I removed myself from his presence. However, we kept in touch about once a week.

I continually asked my guide, "What is the reason for this?" His reply was that I simply was not ready for the answer yet.

About two years later, in one of my meditations, my

guide finally told me that the reason for this encounter was to show me that large amounts of money are available to me without effort; it is just as effortless to have a lot of money as it is to have a little. All that matters is that you believe it is possible, and you believe that you deserve it.

Even though I was prosperous before I met Mustafah, my guide told me that Mustafah was the main reason I was able to extend my abundance and worthiness far beyond what it had ever been. It is such freedom to realize the truth: Mustafah was one of the angels in my life.

WEAKENING THE EGO

As my spirit becomes more empowered by my vigilance for peace and light in my life, my ego becomes weaker and weaker. I am no longer faced with the conflicts that my ego used to thrive on when meeting another ego, because my ego knows that it no longer has my power behind it to win; "It takes two to tango." Giving more power to my Spirit has resulted in no conflicts with other egos.

HOW PROSPERITY WORKS

We had been examining prosperity for several weeks during *A Course in Miracles* seminar, when a man asked me to meet with him after class. He was involved in two businesses and wanted to launch a third, but was in turmoil over his prosperity.

He asked me to back him with several thousand dollars for his new venture, but it was not one in which I wanted to be involved. However, his request did give me the opportunity to explain to him the way prosperity works in our lives.

I told him that "prosperity" does not necessarily mean that we will have hundreds of thousands of dollars sitting idly in the bank. Prosperity is not about greed or excess; it is not about *doing* anything.

Prosperity brings the knowledge and firm belief that everything we need will be provided for us. People who have millions of dollars may not necessarily be prosperous; I may have only a few hundred in the bank, but when I need something, it is always available to me.

MIRACLES ARE NOT SIZED

One morning, as I sat down to write a check for my mortgage payment, I had to admit that this was not one of my favorite pastimes. When I meditated that day, I told my guide that my life was wonderful and that I was living without effort. " . . . except for one thing," I said. "This request would need a big miracle."

"There are no big or small miracles," he interrupted. "Miracles are not sized. What is it that you want?" I told him that I wanted my house mortgage paid. He said that it would be done.

For years, I had been trying to sell a particular piece of commercial property. Unexpectedly, within two months it sold. My commission on the sale was one hundred and four thousand dollars. At first, I was puzzled by the amount, because it exceeded my mortgage. Then, I recognized (with the help of my CPA) that the excess money covered the taxes on my commission.

A LESSON IN FORGIVENESS

Tony is an old friend of mine whom I have known for over twenty years. A few years ago, he asked me to sell his business for him. The very next day, another friend of mine, named Karim, asked me if I had any businesses for sale. When I told him about Tony's, he was very interested and made a full price offer. Tony was elated—he had been willing to accept much less than that. We had a deal. My net commission upon closing would be seventy-five hundred dollars.

A few weeks later, Tony was supposed to meet us at the property and show the business books to Karim. For some reason, however, he did not show up. We made several more appointments to do this, but each time, Tony stood us up. Finally, Karim said that if the seller did not want to sell the business, he was willing to back out. The deal fell through. However, my broker decided that since we had procured a willing and able buyer, we were still entitled to our commission. He then hired an attorney to initiate a lawsuit. When the attorney called me to take my statement, I explained to him that I was unwilling to participate in the lawsuit against Tony. I did not want the commission under those circumstances; I had already forgiven Tony for his behavior. I called my broker and told him of my decision.

Later that day, an Oriental woman whom I had never seen before came to our firm. She walked straight into my broker's office and—for a half-hour—they argued. Needing to ask my broker something that could not wait, I decided to interrupt them. When I opened the door and walked in, the woman stared at me and asked in a very heavy accent, "What is your name?" I told her my name was Bijan. She then said to me, "I see in you . . . you are going to sell my shopping center." My broker turned to me with a surprised look and explained that she had come here to cancel her listing that he had accepted six months earlier and had been unable to sell. Then, she announced to him, "Bijan has the exclusive listing on my property."

What happened next was amazing: I accepted the listing and within forty-eight hours I had a buyer for her property. The deal closed in forty-five days and my net commission was seventy-five thousand dollars!

I knew that by giving up my resentment and grievances against Tony and completely forgiving him, I had literally multiplied my receiving by ten. Although he was not aware of the role he played in my lesson of forgiveness, I was very grateful to Tony.

ASKING FOR WHAT YOU WANT

Shortly after I paid off my automobile, it started to need repairs. The problem was not major, but it was consistent and annoying. One day, when I was worrying about the car, I recalled my guide's advice—simply to ask the Universe for what I wanted.

In my next meditation, I began an involved explanation of why my car was an annoyance—my guide stopped me and suggested that I get to the bottom line, leaving the "*story*" behind. I told him that I wanted a new car. He asked what type and how much. I said that I did not know, but that I would like a four-wheel drive vehicle. He told me to come to him with the definite information, not with a vague request.

Over the next few days, I drove all types of four-wheel drive trucks, including a Samurai, Jeep, Pathfinder, and FourRunner. I went back to my guide and told him that I liked the FourRunner, and that it would be around twenty-four thousand dollars. He told me that it was done.

Within one month, a real estate deal closed in which I had put very little effort. It was unexpected—a gift. I was surprised when I noticed that the amount of the commission was twenty-four thousand dollars.

On the way to purchase my new FourRunner, my ego became very active—after all, I had been in heavy debt only shortly before this. I thought that perhaps I should buy a Jeep and save six thousand dollars—or a Samurai and save half of the money.

In a few minutes, I began to laugh at myself. Even though *I* was coming from prosperity (I had learned my lesson), *ego* was coming from scarcity. The arguments in favor of saving a portion of the money were strong, but ineffective. I ignored my ego, and purchased my FourRunner.

REMEMBERING MY SOURCE

One special day, while I was living in Australia, I walked to a beautiful park to eat my lunch and feed the variety of birds with an extra loaf of bread that I had brought for them. As I sat down on a bench, a half-dozen crows landed in front of me looking for a handout. I gladly reached into my bag and threw a slice onto the ground. All of the crows hungrily dove for the bread, but the first one that reached it snatched the entire slice and flew away with it. Immediately, all of the others took off chasing after the lucky bird. I hurriedly tossed the rest of the slices onto the ground, whistling and shouting to call them back. However, they were determined to get a piece of that stolen bread and were completely oblivious to my invitation. Bewildered, I sat back down on the bench, wondering why they panicked over that one slice. As I thought about their behavior, a feeling of peace overcame me and I realized that this was a profound lesson. Like the crows, I continually ignore the source and try to grab only the measly scraps from others. If I let go of my fear of scarcity, knowing that God is my source, I allow love to remind me that there is always plenty for me and for others to receive. Since that day, I have seen everyone's prosperity in a different light. After my lunch, I walked away with all of the slices of bread still on the ground and no crows in sight.

FORGIVING OTHERS
TO FORGIVE MYSELF

As a real estate agent, I have worked with many different types of people. One time, I placed an ad in the newspaper for the sale of some land. A man who responded to the ad recognized that I spoke with an accent and asked my nationality. When I told him that I was Persian, he began a discussion of the land for sale in my native language. He told me that he had recently moved to Las Vegas from Hawaii, where he owned several businesses. He also owned a nursing home in Las Vegas and had a substantial amount of cash that he wanted to invest in this area. I arranged to take him to lunch. During lunch, he ordered a full meal and several beers. Afterward, we continued to look at properties until dinner time. Again, he told me that he was hungry, and I took him for another meal. As an agent who specializes in rather large land transactions, I am accustomed to taking clients out to eat while putting together land deals, so I wasn't disturbed by his behavior.

During our conversation, he told me that he was fluent in twelve languages, and had degrees in law, dentistry, and oral surgery. Because he spoke many languages, and because of his educational background, he had been employed by the United Nations before his move to Hawaii. As a person who was born in another country, I often meet people who have acquired higher degrees in their native land, then come to the United States and begin another career. During the process, they learn many different languages. He was well-spoken and very knowledgeable. I was honored to be with him and to be of service to him.

Over the next five or six days, our routine remained the same. I would pick him up for breakfast, and we would look at land, go to lunch, search for more land, and finish with dinner. At no time did he offer to pay for anything. In fact, he mentioned that my commission on the sale of the land would far exceed the cost of the meals. Several times he asked me to stop at various places so that he could run personal errands, as well.

Finally, the perfect deal materialized. I wrote up the offer and he gave me a check for ten thousand dollars as a deposit. On my way to the escrow company, he telephoned me on my cellular. He told me that he had cancelled the check and did not want to go ahead with the transaction . . . . I froze. My telephone rang again, and this time it was my girlfriend. When I told her what had happened, she began to laugh at me. I was not pleased. She explained that the man was an accomplished con artist. As a student of *A Course in Miracles*, I looked for the lesson in all of this, but nothing occurred to me. I became angry and upset.

That night, I could not sleep (this is very unusual for me). The fact that I had been misled—not for one day, but for an entire week—was very disturbing. After a restless night, I went to my meditation pyramid with a *big* attitude. One of my guides appeared, laughing at me. I was not amused. I demanded to know what was so funny. After more laughter, he said, "You do not see it, do you?" I explained that I had looked at everything and that there was nothing to see; there was no lesson for me. He suggested that we look at it together. He asked what bothered me the most about it. As I struggled to control my temper, I told him that the man had lied to me about speaking twelve languages. My guide asked me to remember the first day that I had arrived in the United States. A woman had asked me how many languages I spoke. I replied that I spoke six languages, in an attempt to impress her. My guide asked me if that had been true. I told him that it hadn't; I only spoke Persian and marginal English at the time. He began to laugh again and said, "See, he doubled the number of languages that he speaks, so that you could recognize your error and rid yourself of the guilt you have carried for many years. By forgiving him, you forgive yourself."

Only partially relieved, I continued with an outraged reminder that he claimed to have three graduate degrees. After more laughter, my guide asked me to remember my first return trip to Persia—when I had told my family and friends that I was an engineer. Again, my guide asked if *that* had been true. I responded that it hadn't, because I was only in my first year of college at that time. (Until that moment, I had completely forgotten about that one.) My guide resumed his laughter and said, "He *tripled* his degrees, so that you could see your error and rid yourself of the guilt."

Feeling a little embarrassed, I went on to ask about the exaggeration of his cash holdings. By this time, my guide was not laughing and asked me to remember another incident.... This continued until I was in total peace. No longer did I view the client as a con man, but as an angel who had come to rid me of my guilt.

That afternoon, I called my angel and invited him to dinner that evening. I dined with him without animosity or anger. I saw him in a completely different light: as a *savior*. When we parted after dinner, I felt complete with him and at peace with myself. Shortly after that, I telephoned him . . . he had totally disappeared, without a trace.

CAUSE AND EFFECT

Our thoughts are the causes that produce effects, which become our reality. What we see outside of ourselves is only the effect of our thinking. Instead of working to change the effect, we have to work on our mind (our thoughts). It is only at *this* level that change can be made to produce a different effect.

Whenever we produce an effect that we no longer want, it is very important that we accept it as an effect of our own thoughts. Only by *accepting and releasing it* can we be free to create a *different* effect.

For example, suppose that I created a chair, but now decide I no longer want the chair, but a table instead. I must first accept and release the chair (the effect of my thought), before I am free to go back to my mind and create the table.

We can always change the reality outside ourselves by changing our mind about it, and thereby changing the cause!

HONESTY

Three years ago, I purchased a piece of land for a dear friend. A few months later, he asked me to help him sell it. He was willing to take up to a forty-percent loss, just to have a write-off. I understood his urgency and agreed to sell the property.

Later, I realized that the deal was too good to pass up . . . I should buy the land myself. This would help both of us at the same time.

However, I was reluctant to make him the offer and I struggled with it for days. I felt that I would be taking unfair advantage of his situation by purchasing it far below market, then turning around and selling it for the real value.

When we met again, l explained that I had spent many hours trying to put together a deal that would enable me to purchase the land. When I finished, I expected him to be angry and disappointed in me as a friend. His response was amazing. He looked at me in awe and said he wished that he could be that honest. We postponed the decision about the land and spoke instead about honesty and clearing things.

The very next day, I received an offer on the property. It was twice the amount he was willing to sell it for—in fact, he would make a twenty-percent profit! I could not help but tease him as I extended the contract to him with joy.

We both made money and we learned a great lesson: when we are open and honest, Spirit has the opportunity to bring peace and profit.

THE BEAUTY OF THE PRESENT

During my first visit to Australia after my mother's death, I recall wandering around my sister's ranch, completely full of turmoil. Issues of prosperity, combined with homesickness and sadness over my mother's physical absence, had overwhelmed me. My mind was racing from one perceived problem to another; from one area of discontent to the next . . . .

In one moment, I surrendered myself to the present and I let go of all past and future issues. I totally altered the chaos that surrounded me. In doing so, I recognized that there were no past or future complications—indeed, there was only the present.

In that moment, I became aware of the world around me. The beauty of the sights, sounds, and smells was totally and completely overpowering. It was as though I had seen nature in all of its splendor for the first time.

In the present, there was no room for those things of the past because they did not exist—I had created them. In my creation, I had blocked the incomparable beauty of the present.

GRATEFUL SURRENDER

Over the past two years, Kathy and I have come to a very comfortable arrangement regarding the custody of our son, Michael. On five days each week, she brings him to my home at six in the evening. He stays the night, and I return him early in the morning; this gives each of us special time with him. Since they spend the day together, I realize how much she cherishes her two nights a week with Michael.

In 1995, however, I wanted to attend a special event with him that fell on one of those two nights. I telephoned her to ask if Michael could join me for this one evening. I was greeted by a very angry mother. She went into great detail as to why I should not disturb their valued time together. My usual approach would have been to explain patiently why this was a special opportunity and try to persuade her to come to my way of thinking. Instead, I found myself saying, without deliberate attempt to form the words, "You are right. I am sorry. It will not happen again." We said good-bye and I hung up the telephone. I was pleased when I recognized that I was not trying to control the situation.

After about three minutes, the telephone rang . . . it was Kathy. She resumed her explanation, wanting me to fully understand that what I had done was inappropriate, and exactly why I should not have done it. Again, I apologized and humbly hung up the telephone.

Again the telephone rang, and again it was Kathy. This time she wanted me to understand that she was not trying to be mean to me, but did need to make it perfectly clear that I was not to interfere with her time with Michael—under *any* circumstances. I said that I fully understood, and apologized again.

I hung up the telephone, and again the telephone rang. This time she asked me if I really wanted to see him so much that I would disturb their time together. I told her, quite sincerely, that I had made a mistake, I was very sorry, and that it would not happen again.

After another five minutes, the telephone rang again. She said, "Pick him up in about ten minutes . . . but you realize that he doesn't have time to take a shower." I gratefully thanked her, then picked up Michael. As I drove away with him, I realized, once again, that by surrendering control, what I wanted was given to me without effort.

EXCITEMENT IN THE PRESENT

Whenever I am in the present—which is Truth and the only reality—I notice that it is very quiet. Ego says that this is very boring; nothing is happening. But it is not boring; it is really very exciting! The present is about being. When I am there—without my ego and my perception of what it should be like—I am in a place of peace, joy, and love. When I go beyond, to where Truth is, I am where I really want to be.

SERVING MY OWN BEST INTEREST

Prior to starting *A Course in Miracles*, I had studied many enrichment programs that promote seizing control. This is an effective tool for establishing goals, persuading people, and ultimately . . . getting your way. However, the Course teaches that only by relinquishing control to Spirit, will I allow my own best interest to be served. Unfortunately, old habits die hard.

For years, I have regularly gone to a gym to work out. One day, an attractive woman on the Stairmaster caught my eye. I smiled and said, "Hello."

She frowned and muttered a hello in return.

The next day, the same thing happened, but with a different woman. This time, she was even more attractive. Again, I greeted her—and again, I received a scowl and a subdued hello. My ego began a campaign. It reminded me of all the control classes I had taken and encouraged me to go for what I wanted. I surrendered. I jumped on the adjacent Stairmaster and began small-talk. After a half-hour, I asked the woman if she would join me for dinner that evening. She accepted. I was successful; I had gone for it and won . . . . But what had I won?

During dinner, I quickly discovered that we had very

little in common. She smoked, used profanity at every opportunity, and retreated to the rest room frequently. (When she returned each time, she apparently had difficulty with her nose.) Halfway through dinner, I had a raging headache. During one of her rest room visits, I declared to my guide, "Do not EVER listen to me. Give me only what is in my best interest, *not what I ask for!*" After dinner, I used my headache as an excuse to cut our date short and take her home.

The next day at the gym, I walked by the Stairmaster and said hello to the woman using it. It was not my intention to date her; in fact, it was just an absentminded greeting. When she frowned at me and barely said "Hi," I started to laugh inside. I thanked my guide for my lesson—such a complete one.

SHARING THE LESSONS OF OTHERS

During my seven years of studying and teaching *A Course in Miracles*, I continuously expanded my consciousness. On one particular evening, an event happened in our class that brought a lot of light to me.

A few minutes before the end of the session, a friend of mine named Shelly rushed in. She was determined to share her miracle that evening. The class was very full and there were many people still sharing. Finally, it was Shelly's turn. As she excitedly began to speak, another participant named Hannah interrupted and said, "I'm sorry Shelly, class is over now. We can't listen to your miracle tonight."

Everyone was very surprised. Hannah's abruptness seemed out of character—she was a very gentle soul who had a deep love for everyone. I could feel Shelly's disappointment and anger as she rushed out of the room.

Class ended as usual and as everyone exchanged hugs, Hannah came over to me and broke down crying in my arms. "What have I done? What would make me act so mean to Shelly? Why didn't I give her the opportunity to share?" she asked pleadingly.

"God works in mysterious ways," I said. "Many

times, things that we believe are hurtful are really done for our own best interest. When we open our minds to the knowledge that there is always another way to view any experience in life, we can begin to recognize everything as good."

Five days later, I received a phone call from Shelly. I could hear the excitement in her voice. "I've been in so much turmoil since I left that night," she said. "But I just got off the phone with my friend Nancy, and I now realize that what happened that night was really a miracle for me!

When Nancy asked me how I reacted when I couldn't share my miracle, I told her that I felt totally out of control and just ran away. Then Nancy asked me, 'But isn't that what you do with all of your relationships whenever you feel out of control?'"

By this time, Shelly was crying with joy. "All these years I never understood why my relationships failed. I am so thankful for having been at your class that night and for the confrontation with that wonderful woman. She helped me to bring my awareness to a level where I could finally see the truth. I'd like to phone her and express my deepest gratitude and thanks—I'm sure that she doesn't realize what she did for me."

While I was giving her Hannah's number, I became

aware that there was a beautiful lesson in all of this for me too: When I come from love, it does not matter what the circumstances may look like to me; there is always a profound effect on someone else's life as well as mine. In every action, there is always a lesson for someone. I do not need to concern myself with the outcome. I just need to remind myself to *trust God.*

SURRENDERING CONTROL

I am routinely reminded of the advantages of surrendering control. Last week, for example, I purchased two finches (a male and a female) with the intention of breeding them. Yesterday, to my surprise, both finches were singing (females do not sing).

This morning, I telephoned the gentleman who sold them to me and explained the situation. I was eager to resolve the problem and hoped to replace one of the males with a female as soon as possible.

He told me that he had a medical appointment in ninety minutes. I was about to convince him that, if I hurried, I could make it to his house quickly enough for him to exchange the bird and still arrive at his appointment on time. But before I spoke, I caught myself.

Instead, I agreed to the time that he suggested later in the afternoon. I was actually surprised by my response, since I firmly believed that I had plenty of time to make the exchange.

After I spoke with him, I received a telephone call from an appointment that I thought was scheduled later in the day. The gentleman reminded me that I was to see him in fifteen minutes. (This was a two-part real estate meeting that was very important—I had inadvertently written only the second half of the meeting in my planner.)

Had I insisted upon controlling the time to exchange the finches, I would have been unavailable to attend this important and profitable meeting.

SEEING THE TRUTH ABOUT
MYSELF THROUGH OTHERS

A short while after studying *A Course in Miracles,* I had the opportunity to heal my perception of a colleague. I was not very happy working with him and I never felt good about myself while I was in his presence.

There were only two choices available to me: I could either leave the company, or I could try to get along with him. I chose to stay and asked my guide for help.

"Imagine that you are a loving father with a lot of children, or a master with many loyal students," he said. "When a child or student comes to you asking for help or calling for love, what do you do? Everyone you meet or have contact with is your child or your student asking you 'Who Am I?' Your function in this world is to see beyond their behavior and tell them who they really are: powerful children of God—lights of the world. As they will know this truth, they will mirror back to you who you really are as well. You cannot do it by yourself."

The very next day, I found myself excited about going to work and healing my perception about this individual. When I arrived at my office and was contemplating him verbally attacking me, to my surprise, all that I saw was a loving person who just wanted to share his love and light with me in the best way that he could.

Since that moment, I have found him to be funny and joyous; I have felt very peaceful in his presence.

LOVE OR DISCIPLINE

When my son Michael was about four years old, he would often come to visit. His method of getting my attention was to pull on my ears, grab my clothes, and annoy me. When this behavior became intolerable, I would regain control with the age-old technique of shaking him harshly.

One night, Michael began repeating his pattern of misbehaving. As I held him in the moment before I started to shake him, a beautiful miracle occurred. I saw my real self as God's son. Instead of shaking Michael, I held him close to me. As I looked into his eyes, I told him that I loved him, and kissed him. This behavior was totally unprecedented—we had always shared a "macho" relationship. His response was equally unusual. He gently caressed my cheek in a very loving fashion. We gazed deeply into each other's eyes as we wept. Slowly, my son's physical body began to fade. As I held him, he was transformed into a bright light. It seemed as though we were in that moment for an eternity. Since then, my relationship with Michael has been permanently altered. I no longer need to control him with physical means.

JUDGMENT

At the end of either the second or third *A Course in Miracles* meeting I attended, I noticed that one of the ladies was using the study book as a footrest. This was uncomfortable for me because I felt that it was disrespectful to treat it in this manner. I saw it as holy . . . like the Bible, the Torah, or the Koran.

I approached the woman and said, "Using the book in this way is very disrespectful because it contains the word of God."

She smiled and replied, "That is your perception."

I really did not understand what she was saying, so I continued, insisting that she should apologize, pick up the book, and treat it with more respect.

Again she smiled and said, "It is only a book."

It took me a while to realize what she meant. With my judgment, I make things *more* or *less* important. When the name of God is in a book, only *my* judgment can make the book holier than anything or anyone else. Through this experience, I noticed that once I clear my judgment out of the way, everything is equal and perfect.

TRAFFIC MIRACLES

One day, while driving the freeway in Las Vegas, I pulled behind some very slow traffic in the exit lanes. As the traffic in my lane began to move again, a car in the fast lane suddenly pulled into the few feet of space that opened between my car and the vehicle in front of me. I barely stopped in time to avoid hitting him, and consequently, the vehicle behind me barely missed my car—I was outraged! Surely my anger was not the appropriate response. So I asked my guide, "What is the lesson in all of this?"

I heard a voice clearly say, "Look at the driver in front of you." As I looked, I could see that he was trying very hard not to glance at me in his rearview mirror.

Again I asked, "Please clarify this."

The voice said, "Remember last week, when you were in a hurry and pulled in front of someone?"

I remembered that incident clearly, and that I was also trying very hard not to glance at the driver behind me in my rearview mirror. As I opened my vision, I could see that every incident that occurred on that off-ramp had been *me* at one time or another.

The voice concluded by saying, "If you give up

worrying about time, you will realize how perfect everything in the Universe is."

Since that day, I have changed my perception. I find that whenever I am in that slow lane, I gladly open a space and give way to "myself in another car." In fact, I go out of my way to smile and show forgiveness to "myself in the other car" whenever *I* do something that is inconsiderate. Life is great when you get in touch with who you are!

REMEMBERING MY GOAL

I was Mr. Universe, Natural Division, in 1993 and 1994. I trained for the competitions and looked good. In November 1995, I represented the United States at the World Cup of Bodybuilding, Natural Division, in Australia. I finished in Second Place; First Place went to an Australian. When he was named the winner, I was very happy for him—after all, it was his home and he had many friends and relatives at the competition. I returned to Las Vegas and continued to train. As the Mr. Universe competition in December approached, I was confident that I would win again. With the additional training and preparation for Australia, I had never looked better.

When I went to the prejudging for the competition in California, I realized that there were two men who would finish ahead of me. (As a former judge, I knew the criteria for winning.) I felt angry, and was convinced that they had used steroids. I was tired and not my usual enthusiastic self. After the prejudging, my son Michael and I returned to our room. I asked him to be quiet while I meditated.

My guide came to me quickly. I explained that I was feeling weak and very upset; I was confused and believed that I was being cheated. I asked him how I could have won the title last year, but might lose it this year.

He asked me what my goal was in this world. I responded, without hesitation, "Peace." He asked me if I had altered my goal . . . . I immediately understood: My goal *now* was to be Mr. Universe. My guide continued to explain to me that if I won this year, I would continue to pursue the Mr. Universe title. I realized that in my quest to be Mr. Universe, I had sacrificed my peace: If we live in turmoil, we do not miss peace; but if we have known peace, its absence is profound.

After my meditation, I felt strong, happy, and peaceful. Although I normally do not eat between the prejudging and the finals, Michael and I went out for a big Persian feast. When we returned, I sought out the two men who I thought would finish ahead of me. I told them that they looked magnificent, and *should* win the competition. They were shocked at my attitude change—my son was even more puzzled! He said that I was a totally different person from who I had been at the prejudging. It is so great to be at peace.

GIFT FROM A FRIEND

My long time best friend shared a story with me which illustrates, very clearly, the importance of our point of view.

One Friday, while driving, he passed a hitchhiker. Although he was not in the habit of stopping, when he noticed that it was a woman alone, he offered her a ride. As they chatted, he realized how much they had in common and that she was very pretty. He asked her if she would like to have something to eat and she accepted.

After dinner, they drove to her neighborhood. She said that she did not want her mother to worry about her hitchhiking, so she asked him to drop her off down the street. He asked if she would like to see him again. She said that she was busy over the weekend, but that he could call her on Monday.

Throughout the weekend, he was happy in anticipation of seeing her again. The more he thought about her, the lovelier she became.

On Monday, he waited until the afternoon to call her. When he dialed the number, he was greeted with the recording "This number is no longer in service."

Later, when he told me the story, I rallied to his side and expressed dismay at how disappointed he must have felt. He chuckled and explained to me that he had two choices. Certainly, he could have dwelt upon disappointment; but instead, he chose to bless her for the pleasant weekend he spent in anticipation of seeing her again. It was all in his point of view—his outlook. She was still a lovely lady.

HAVING GOALS

Because this world is very goal oriented, it seems impossible to live without having them. So we are always setting various goals for ourselves to achieve. However, if we make peace our goal and have no others, everything that we need to achieve the goal of peace will be given to us. If we need good health to have peace, good health will be ours. If we need a great relationship to have peace, that will also be provided for us. We always reach our goal because God gives us what we want. What is most important is our choice of which goal to pursue. To have a joyous and effortless life, our only goal must be peace.

GIFTS FROM THE FATHER

My son asked me for a new video game that has been the talk of all the boys in school. He said that he would be forever grateful if I would get it for him. His deep desire and persistence made me more than happy to buy the game. However, what I noticed after he had it was very interesting. He soon began to spend most of his waking hours with it. He no longer had any time for his homework, his daily chores, or me.

I decided to ask my guide which approach I should take to correct him. My guide asked me, "What is he doing that you do not like?" I replied that he had made a god out of his video game. He smiled and said, "Isn't that what you do with most of the gifts that you receive from your Father? You are so persistent with what you want—and you want it all. With deep desire you always say, 'I will be forever grateful if you give me this gift.' Soon after you have it, however, you make that gift your god. This is not only true of ego's wishes, but also true whenever you receive the part of your inheritance that is prosperity, health, and effortless relationships. You serve these gifts so loyally that you completely forget about your Father. Remember that your goal is peace, while your function in this world is to heal yourself and others." Once again, an experience with my son has taught me a valuable lesson.

PROJECTING MY GUILT

My ex-wife Kathy and I were together for about three years. She is a magnificent person and I have learned many lessons from her. For a time during our marriage, we lived with my mother in Australia. One day, when I came home from the gymnasium, I found my mother in the kitchen. She had just returned from the market. As I approached her, I noticed that she was washing the plastic grocery bags to reuse them. A sense of disappointment came over me. I thought to myself, "With all of the money that I make and the income that she receives, why would she have to do that?" I was just about to scold her when Kathy walked up to me.

"What's the matter? Why are you upset?" she asked. I explained the situation and how I felt. Kathy started to laugh, but I was not amused. Then she reminded me of an incident that had occurred two days earlier . . . .

Kathy and I had been in the kitchen and my mother walked in. When she noticed that I was holding an empty grocery bag, she said to me, "Don't throw that away!"

As soon as she said that, my ego stepped right in. "Mother, we don't need to save these bags," I said, throwing the bag away—though I really had every intention of saving it.

I smiled at Kathy and acknowledged the miracle: I had become upset with my mother because I did not feel good about myself doing the exact same thing that she had done (saving the grocery bags). Like her, I had come from a place of scarcity—and I felt guilty about it. Not wanting or liking the guilt, I projected it onto my mother. Only by seeing it in someone else, was I able to bring it up to be healed in me. Once I realized this, I could easily forgive myself while I was forgiving her. Instead of scolding my mother, I kissed her and told her how much I loved her.

LOVE DOES NOT PUNISH

Yesterday I received a copy of my son Michael's report card from his school. I was surprised by his low grades and decided to give him a call. I wanted to express my love for him as well as my acceptance. He was not very happy to hear from me and asked why I had called. I told him that I wanted to tell him that I love him. Then he asked if I had received his report card. I told him that I had, and that I knew he would do better next time. I also told him that it was important for him to let go of the past. He asked me if that was really why I had called. I told him that I called simply to tell him that I loved him.

"Well, my mom loves me too," he said.

"Of course she does," I assured him.

"She loves me more than you do," he continued.

"I know that she loves you unconditionally, as I do," I stated, rather confused by his remark. "We both love you very much."

"No, my mom loves me *a lot* more than you do," he added. "I know that she does because she was very upset about my grades. She even punished me by taking away my computer and television privileges. That's why I know that she loves me more than you do."

Still confused by his perception, I decided to let it go. I again told him that I loved him and said good night. I went to my meditation table to meditate and my guide came up quickly. I asked him how my son could believe that I didn't love him because I didn't want to punish him or make him feel guilty about his grades. My love for him has always been unconditional.

My guide explained to me that Michael's belief system, like that of so many people on this planet, associates love with punishment. He said, "When they have done something that they or others judge to be incorrect or improper, they feel guilty. To relieve their guilt they must be punished. In their eyes, the one who punishes them is the one who loves them." He continued, "Many of you feel the same way about God. You feel abandoned or believe that He doesn't love you because He doesn't punish you when you have done something that you feel guilty about. Because you grew up believing in the 'wrath of God', you have an image of your Father as vengeful, angry and judgmental. But your Father is none of these things. He is like the sun; He shines light everywhere. He cannot shine darkness. He is only capable of shining the light of unconditional love and joy, which He is. And He sees you as He created you: loving, joyful and magnificent. Anger, judgment and vengeance are darkness. And all darkness comes from the ego."

This lesson was very powerful for me. I began to see that whenever I had judged myself as not good enough, unworthy, undeserving and guilty, I had created the need within me to be punished. Since my Father wouldn't punish me, I had attracted other egos that would contribute to me by punishing me and making me suffer. By resolving my guilt through punishment, my ego had been justified and I could continue to do the same thing over and over.

The truth is that our Father is love, joy, peace and happiness. He loves us unconditionally and He does not punish us. Only we can bring forth the punishment that we feel we deserve.

Today when I picked my son up from school, I told him that I wanted to share the powerful miracle that had come as a result of our conversation the night before. He was very open and he listened carefully. When I was finished, he hugged me and said that it was true. Whenever he had done something that he thought was wrong, he had waited to be punished, believing that punishment was a form of love and caring. But after hearing my powerful miracle, he could see how I had been unwilling to contribute to his guilt. Realizing this, he now understood that by not judging him, I was extending unconditional love and acceptance.

The more I share my miracles with my son, the more wonderful and holy our relationship becomes. Since I do not judge him as being "too young", or incapable of receiving the knowledge, he is also given the opportunity to grow from the lessons I am learning.

Every day I thank God for the blessings that come from communicating openly and honestly with other human beings.

SEEING THROUGH THE EYES
OF LOVE

In late 1988, on one of the trips to visit my mother and sister in Australia, an incredible miracle happened. I was at the airport waiting to board my Quantas flight when I noticed an old woman across the way. She reminded me of the witch in Snow White. She had small beady eyes, a long chin, and a very large nose with a wart on the end. Her hair looked dirty and stringy and she seemed to be scowling. When I became aware of how strong my judgment was about her, I felt uncomfortable and was in turmoil over it—until I remembered that how I saw anyone or anything was up to me. I knew that I was always able to control how I perceived things simply by choosing to see them differently.

I decided that a shift in perception was needed to bring me back to peace. I closed my eyes and began to imagine that she was my mother, who has unconditional love for me. I thought about my childhood . . . how my mother would hug and kiss me and comfort me when I was hurt. As I continued to remember my mother, I felt a deep love and appreciation for this woman.

When I opened my eyes, I was surprised to see how different the woman looked to me. Her eyes were bright and sparkling. Her face had a glow about it and a huge smile that I had not seen before. As I looked at her, she waved at me to come and sit next to her. "I have brought some home cooking with me," she whispered. "Come sit over here and we can enjoy the food together." Immediately, I was filled with overwhelming love. I literally wanted to hug and kiss her.

For the next hour we ate, laughed, and told jokes. In my eyes, she had become one of the most beautiful women I had ever met. A deep sadness came over me as she left to board the plane at the gate next to mine.

That lovely woman brought me such a powerful miracle: I realized how quickly my perception could change once I was willing to forgo judgment and bring forth unconditional love. As I allowed myself to see who she truly was—a perfect child of God— her beautiful self was able to shine through and I found my way home to peace. I never saw her again, but I will never forget her smiling face and loving heart.

LETTING GO OF WHAT I WANT

Recently, my son Michael invited a couple of his friends over. After we picked up the two boys from their homes, they sat in the back seat, while Michael sat in front with me. Over the past few years, I have been holding Michael's hand whenever he is in the car with me; he enjoys the unconditional love and warmth that we have for each other as much as I do. This time, however, when I held out my hand to take his, he tried not to be noticed by his friends as he gently shook his head and very quietly said, "No." I really wanted to hold his hand, so I opened my hand to him one more time and winked at him. Again, he shook his head, looking a little uncomfortable about the situation. "No," he insisted.

I gave up trying to persuade him; I gave up control of what I wanted and said to myself, "Let it be as it is." Then, I realized that Michael and his friends were around eleven years old: the age when they do not want to be seen as dependent upon their parents. Therefore, I felt that it was quite all right for me to just sit there and drive.

About half way home, one of Michael's friends asked me, "Mr. Anjomi, were you Mr. Universe in 1993 and 1994?"

I replied, "Yes."

He said that he would be very happy to have a father with the title of Mr. Universe. Then he turned to Michael and said, "You are so lucky to have a father who is so nice to you—and who was Mr. Universe!"

Suddenly, Michael put his hand out and snapped his fingers, saying, "Daddy—hand, hand." I put out my hand and he held it very, very tightly. He explained to his friends how much we love each other and how much he appreciates me. He also told them that we hold hands as we ride in the car because we are so close and have such a good relationship. Both of the boys thought it was "awesome."

That day, the most important lesson for me was to give up control by not insisting that Michael hold my hand. I just allowed it to happen by itself.

Whenever I put out my thought of what I want and let it go (instead of using my ego to persuade someone to do what I want them to do), whatever is good for me and the situation will happen automatically and effortlessly. It will also bring a healing to the relationship. I felt good about that day. I had a wonderful time with the boys and enjoyed myself.

THE LOVE OF GOD

A Course in Miracles says that if you take someone you love most in this world and multiply that love by a hundred times and then multiply that love by a thousand times, you will get only a glimpse of how much your Father loves you.

I wanted to try this so that I could know how it felt. I meditated and brought forth my love for my son, Michael. I multiplied my unconditional love for him by two, and then by three, and so on. By the time I got to six, I could not multiply it any higher . . . . My love was so strong and of such high quality that I had to see Michael and be with him every second of the day. I realized from my experience of multiplying my love for my son that I could not begin to comprehend the magnitude of my Father's love for me. I felt so safe and so loved in His hands, that it put me in a state of total ecstasy and joy.

THE PATH OF LIFE

In 1990, after I had been studying *A Course in Miracles* for over a year, I entered a six-month period of heavy meditation and growth. During that time, I was not involved in a relationship. One morning, after finishing my workout, I told my guide that it was about time for me to start dating someone. As I was leaving, I noticed two women entering the gym. Although we had never met, I greeted them, and we chatted for a few minutes. At the end of the conversation, one of the women gave me her telephone number. Later, I called her and we went to dinner. As we got to know each other, I realized how compatible we were. The relationship began effortlessly and continued that way for over three years. During that time, we both experienced many miracles.

However, the relationship changed as time went on. Although we had previously enjoyed a very powerful, non-judgmental, loving experience, we had now become critical of one another. Just as she became jealous of my time with my son, I became aggravated by her time on the telephone while she was with me; we no longer enjoyed being in the present together. Within two months, we broke up twice and then got back together. During our third and final breakup, my greatest miracle occurred.

A friend of mine who owned a nightclub suggested that I come to work there on weekend nights for a few hours. One Friday evening, my former girlfriend came into the club with several of her friends. I welcomed them and hugged her. During the evening, she was joined by a man. They sat very close to where I was working and soon the two of them began to hold hands and kiss. I experienced great turmoil when I saw her with someone else. To ease my discomfort, I moved to another area of the club. After a couple of hours, I noticed that her friends were preparing to leave. When I asked them where she had gone, they said that she had left with the man. I felt confused and in pain.

That Friday, I had one of my rare sleepless nights. When I went to my meditation pyramid, I asked my guide for a way to peace. He told me to imagine myself on life's path, content and peaceful until I came to a body of water. To cross the water, I needed a boat—in this case, *she* was the boat. It took her over three years to carry me to the other side. During this effortless voyage, there was tremendous growth and there were many miracles. However, when we reached our destination, our journey together was over. After landing, I was supposed to continue on my path. Then he asked me, "But did you do that? No." He continued by explaining that when I was on the land, I remembered how much fun my boat voyage had been, so I would get back on the boat.

But once aboard, I would realize that we were not going anywhere. Again, I would disembark. This pattern repeated itself until I finally decided to continue along my path . . . . But I did so by walking backwards and gazing at the boat. I would look to see who else got on, how she treated him, and how he treated her. My guide concluded by saying, "Bijan, you cannot see what is in front of you by walking backwards." I was filled with peace.

The next night, she returned to the club and met him there. As they passed by me to leave, she pulled her hand out of his. I walked up to them, introduced myself to him, and hugged her. I told him that she was a wonderful woman—I had no animosity or anger. I felt great love and appreciation toward her for the journey that we had taken together.

UNFORTUNATE CIRCUMSTANCES ... OR GIFTS?

Often, my ego comes up shouting and screaming over what seem to be unfortunate circumstances. Although I may not recognize them as gifts at first, they always are. For example, when I have an appointment or a date that doesn't show up, I accept it as a gift from God, knowing that neither of them would have been in my best interest. And if I were to get fired from my job, I would know that it is because there is a better one waiting for me. The bottom line is that I trust God. I know that all of this is happening for my growth and is absolutely a gift for me.

HEALING MY PERCEPTIONS

Over the years, I have healed my perception of hundreds of people in the gym. But the one who stands out the most is a man named Jack; he was unfriendly to everyone. The first time I saw him, I walked up, extended my hand and said, "Good morning, my name is Bijan."

He gave me a cold look and very calmly said, "I know," then walked away. Immediately, my ego stepped in and tried to convince me that I was wasting my time. I refused to listen.

Every morning, I would say "Hi," and he would ignore me. After about four months of persistence, he finally acknowledged me quietly by nodding his head. I knew that I had made progress and from that point on, every time I said "Good morning," he would nod his head.

One day, I walked up to him, put my hand out and said, "Good morning, my name is Bijan."

He shook my hand and replied, "My name is Jack." He explained that he was somewhat shy and did not like to talk to people in the gym. I acknowledged that, thanked him, and walked away.

About two years later, while talking to some friends

at the gym, Jack walked in. The minute he saw me, he said, "Good morning, Bijan," with a big smile on his face. My friends were quite surprised. They admitted to me that this was the first time they had ever seen him act that friendly toward anyone. I was very pleased. Once again, I was reminded of how much I can heal my perception and grow when I am vigilant for the light, and not for the ego.

DECISION MAKING IN THE PRESENT

I find that in making any decision, the information I most often want to use comes from the past—from my ego. But to make the decision that will bring me peace, I must forget the past and decide without those judgments. This is very hard for me to do; sometimes I panic and want to rely on information from the past. Yet whenever I stay in the present and make my decision from that moment, asking God for guidance, the result is always great—even magnificent!

LOOKING BEYOND JUDGMENT

A few years ago, I decided to start healing my mind about people in the gym. I began by greeting anyone whom I had any kind of judgment toward. One of the most interesting episodes happened with a man who was tall, very big, incredibly masculine, and covered with tattoos. With his baseball cap turned backwards, he looked like a gang member who just got out of prison and was ready to hurt someone. I thought to myself, "Oh, no. Now I have to greet him and heal my mind about *this* judgment."

The man walked over to the heavyweight part of the gym and started to set up the bench press machine with the free weights. He had several of the weights on each side—more than I had seen anyone else use. As I walked closer to him, he started to work out, making loud groaning and moaning noises that sounded very dangerous and scary. I told myself, "Well, I can handle this some other time . . . when it's more appropriate."

But a voice said, "You have given your word to clear any judgment, and this is a judgment."

I took another step closer and then recalled that serious bodybuilders do not appreciate people bothering them while they are working out. Again, I said to myself, "No problem. I can see him when he is finished . . . tomorrow, or some other day."

The voice said, "You have given your word . . . do not break your word."

With hesitation and an uncomfortable feeling, I slowly walked over to him as he completed his set. I extended my hand and said, "Hello, my name is Bijan." I did not know what kind of reaction to expect from him since he definitely did not look happy or friendly. To my complete surprise, he put his hand out and shook mine very warmly.

"My name is Dan," he said.

As we started talking, I told him that he looked very strong and that he must have been working out for a long time. He said that he had been in several competitions, but only placed second, third, or fifth—never first. I told him that this did not have anything to do with his size, how defined he was, or how he looked; it was all about *allowing* himself to receive the First-Place trophy. He seemed very interested in what I had to say and invited me to sit down (this is not something that bodybuilders do in the middle of a work out). We ended up having a warm conversation for almost thirty minutes. He was pleasant and very respectful. When we finished and I went on my way, I had total love for this man and felt that he was one of the nicest people I had ever met. I laughed at myself, relieved to see how my perception changes whenever I am willing to look beyond my judgment.

About four days later, I saw Dan again. He had the same frown on his face as he did before, except this time he was also wearing dark glasses. My work out partner said, "Oh, no—look at *that* guy." When he saw me, he took off his glasses and waved—but by the time I waved back, he already had his glasses back on, and the same frown was on his face again. No matter what my friend thought, I knew that under Dan's frown was a gentle and warm man that I felt a deep love for.

A PROBLEM WITH MEN

Not long ago, I realized that I get along much better with women than I do with men. With deep thought and meditation, I found that there is a very easy way to correct the situation: Since I love myself, my father, and my son, all that I have to do is see myself in any men who are around my age, see my father in anyone older than I am, and see my son in anyone younger than I. Once I started to see men this way, miraculously, the problem was resolved. I no longer have a problem with men.

OUR FUNCTION

I have been studying *A Course in Miracles* religiously every day for several years. Once in a while I find myself asking the same question: "Why don't I feel the presence of God inside of me at every moment? Deep down, I know that I am always with Him and that He and I are communicating continuously." Then I remembered that the Course says that only a very small fraction of who we are is caught up in this dream of separation; and in this confusion and darkness we have created the world. Needing more clarity, I decided to ask my guide, "Why am I more in touch with this thought of separation, which is so small, rather than with the much larger part of me that is connected to the Father?"

He explained with this example: "When you have a sore thumb, all of your attention goes to your thumb—you literally become your thumb. Your life with your Father is so effortless that it does not demand any attention. However, all of the healing and forgiveness has to be applied in this life to lighting up the darkness, or (in this example) healing your sore thumb. We always apply healing to where it is needed the most." He said that the guilt I have in my mind is only a small part of a huge deposit, which lies in my subconscious. To heal it, I must bring it up piece by piece. I do this by projecting it onto someone else so that I can see it in myself. As I forgive and heal that person, I forgive and heal myself as well. That is why our function in this world is to heal ourselves and others—nothing else. Everything that we do (our relationships, our jobs, our dreams as we sleep, and our interactions with everyone) is a stepping stone and an opportunity to do our function.

WHERE WE DO GOD'S WORK

From the time I was a young boy of nine or ten years old, I have admired my older brother Michael's body. He was a devoted bodybuilder and used to pose for me. When I was about thirteen, I began to train at the gym. Since then, working out has become a part of my daily life. Today, many studies outline the benefits of working out and the chemicals that are released in the process . . . but all that I knew was that I felt good and working out was as natural to me as eating and sleeping.

After years of lifting weights, I yearned for the time when I could participate in some significant bodybuilding competitions. However, I was aware that I would need to use steroids to achieve the muscle mass necessary to compete successfully. Since I was definitely not interested in using drugs to alter my body, I just let it go. Shortly after that, in January 1993, I learned of several natural contests, including the big one: Mr. Universe, Natural Division Competition. All participants are screened by blood tests, urinalysis, and/or lie detector. In February 1993, I entered and won the Nevada competition; in April, the California; in June, the U.S.; and in December 1993, my first Mr. Universe title.

Is bodybuilding my life? Most certainly not. The role of bodybuilding became very clear to me one evening during *A Course in Miracles* seminar. One of the other students challenged my suggestion that we should move beyond the body to seek the love and light within ourselves. He demanded to know how I could say that, when I was obviously very involved in building *my own* body. I was stunned . . . I had never thought of myself in that way.

My response was spontaneous—and to this day reflects my honest feelings about my body, working out, and the gym. I explained that the gym offers me an abundance of miracles. On a daily basis, I am presented with many opportunities to practice *A Course in Miracles*—in fact, several of my colleagues from the gym have joined me at the seminar on Monday nights. Even my titles facilitate growth in the gym: because of them, people will approach me and inquire about fitness and training. This often opens the door for my functions of healing, loving, and forgiving. Who are we to question where God guides us to do His work?

ON THE DEATH OF A LOVED ONE

I have always been extremely close to my mother. She and I have a connection that I have not shared with anyone else. While she was alive, I appreciated her counsel as much as her wit. Each year I would travel to Australia to see her. Above all others, she marked my spiritual growth as I studied *A Course in Miracles*.

In the fall of 1992, she came to the United States for a visit. While here, she decided to travel to Calgary, Canada to see an old friend. My plan was that she would return and spend a few weeks with me in Las Vegas. In November, I received a very somber telephone call from my brother, John. He told me that Mother had suffered a heart attack. I was not distressed; instead, I treated it lightly. Perhaps even then I knew it was all perfect. He continued, "No, it is *really* serious—she is in a coma." He asked me to meet him in Canada.

When I arrived at the hospital, four hours after John, I walked into a room where a body lay. It was hooked up to tubes and machines. I recognized the body as my mother, but she was definitely not occupying it. The doctor explained to us that we could request that the machines be disconnected. However, without our request, she would have to remain on them for several more days. I advised the doctor that we would let him know. I told John that Mother was no longer in her body. He looked puzzled. I said that she would want us to have some fun and enjoy the city, since we would not be back here again. He looked bewildered and asked if I was sure of this. I asked him if it was not what Mom would want us to do. He agreed that it was. Then I spoke to our mother. I told her that we wanted her to come back if she could. But if she could not, I wanted her to send us a sign to let her go. As we left the hospital, John asked again if I was sure. "Let's go," I said, "Mom is not here." We went downtown and enjoyed ourselves as best we could.

The next day, we returned to the hospital. Mother was in the same condition—the nurses said that nothing had changed. I asked if something happened during the night, but each nurse said that nothing had. John looked at me and said, "Maybe she didn't hear you,"—but I knew that she had. We waited for the doctor. His report was the same as the nurses'. Again, I inquired if something had occurred. He asked me how I knew, and then went on to explain that, without apparent cause, all of the machines had stopped in the night . . . . We had our answer.

John and I decided to call our sister Terry, before instructing the doctor to disconnect the life support. Terry told us to do whatever we felt was best. After we spoke to the doctor, we went to a mortuary to make the arrangements. Our options included cremation, burial in Canada, or shipping her somewhere else for burial. John and I were inclined toward cremation. As we were discussing our decision, I became aware that Mother wanted to be buried next to my late brother, Michael and his two sons. When I talked about this with John, he immediately agreed.

We told the mortician of our decision. He offered to check the availability of flights on which her body could be shipped. When he returned a few minutes later, the news was not good. There were no flights available to San Jose, California for the next five days. Since John and I were leaving that evening, we were uncomfortable with her body remaining in Canada. As we were packing in the hotel room, the telephone rang. It was the mortician. He told us, with amazement, that he had received notification from the airlines that there was cargo space available that evening—and, to our surprise, it was on John's flight.

When John contacted the San Jose cemetery to make the arrangements for Mother, he was told that the plot next to Michael's was not available and the closest one was across the way. Disappointed, we decided to take it. On the day that Mother was to be buried, John received a telephone call from the funeral director informing him that the person who owned the grave next to Michael's had defaulted. The site next to my brother was now available.

From the morning after my mother left her body, she has joined me in my regular meditations. Each day, her presence continues to give me guidance and love.

HEALING

All people are capable of healing, as long as they are not fearful. To become healers, they must first relinquish control, realizing that they themselves are not doing the healing. Instead, the natural healing is done by the Universe through them, as the healers recognize their oneness with the persons being healed. In this joining, both parties benefit. Although I did not plan to become a healer, I read in *A Course in Miracles* that it is natural for us to heal—it is our function in this world.

I was working in a nightclub when I first started to do healing. I would relieve the headaches of colleagues who suffered from the loud noise. On many occasions, the bartender would refer people to me when they requested aspirin. Although the process was not something that I controlled, I soon became sensitive to when the healing was complete because a tremendous sense of peace would overcome me. However, I could only heal people if they *wanted* to be healed.

After several months of experience in healing, I met a trainer at the gym. His knee was wrapped and he was obviously in a lot of pain. I asked about his injury. He told me the extent of the problem in medical terms that I did not understand. I asked if he wanted to be healed. "Of course," he replied (he was scheduled for surgery in two days). We held hands and I felt myself enter his body. While I was there, I vaguely recognized his pain. I asked the Father to heal me. Once back in my own body, I was overcome with the tremendous sense of peace. As we dropped our hands, he remarked that his pain had subsided, and that he could move around freely, without discomfort. When he went to his physician for his preoperative visit, he was advised that surgery was no longer necessary.

A few weeks later, a woman at the gym with a neck injury came to see me—the trainer had sent her. She was facing a difficult back surgery and was in great pain. I asked if she wanted to be healed. When she said that she did, we went to a corner of the gym and held hands. I felt myself enter her body, and actually felt my own neck being pulled to one side; I was now sharing her pain. Once again, I asked the Father to heal me . . . . When the tremendous peace overcame me, we separated. She was amazed that her pain was gone. Her first question was, "Do I still have to have this surgery?" I told her that she needed to consult her doctor. Her second question was the one most often asked of me: "What did you do?" To this day, I really do not know how the healing occurs, I simply know that *it is not of me.*

GUIDED BY SPIRIT

As we were growing up, we were taught the importance of being in control; the more control that we had, the happier we would be. The truth is that the more we surrender control to Spirit (taking it away from ego), the more we will be guided in the right direction. It is like jumping into a river while wearing a life jacket. As we float downstream near the rocks, we can try to push ourselves away, but we will usually crash into them. However, if we just let go and let the water carry us through, it will naturally take us around the rocks. If we just give up control, with little intention of going anywhere other than where the current leads, we will be carried where we are supposed to go, and where it will be best for us.

IF YOU WANT TO KNOW WHAT YOU WANT, LOOK AT WHAT YOU HAVE

Whenever you're unhappy about an experience in your life, remember that on some level you have asked for the experience and accepted it for yourself. In order to change what you will receive, completely release what you do not want and ask for what you really want. The Universe will fulfill your wishes to the degree that you keep your word in your life (see *Keeping Your Word* p. 43).

EFFORTLESS PROSPERITY
GLOSSARY

EFFORTLESS PROSPERITY — Prosperity is having not only financial abundance, but also perfect relationships and excellent health. Without all of these things, we cannot be in peace. When we are in peace, we have prosperity in *every* area of our lives.

Living a life of effortless prosperity is about "*being*" in the present. In the present moment, we are totally provided for as precious children of God. We do not have to "*do*" anything that comes from ego in order to be effortlessly prosperous; miracles show up constantly and effortlessly. We become the creators of our universe, manifesting everything we ask for. To have effortless prosperity is to be in total peace.

EGO — Ego is the part of the mind that mis-creates. It loves darkness and turmoil and stories about darkness and turmoil. It lives in the *guilt* of the past and the *fear* of the future. Ego blocks and denies our ability to bring forth our inheritance from our Creator; it undermines our attempts to grow to higher levels through its denial of our inner goodness. Ego speaks to us in the language of criticism, judgment, insecurity, scarcity, separation, sacrifice, and fear. When we listen to ego, turmoil is always the result.

EXTENSION — Extension is the way in which God creates. He extended Himself and created us. When we share our love, we are extending as God does.

FUNCTION — Our function is our mission while we are here on earth. It is to heal ourselves and others through love and forgiveness.

HEALING — Healing is our function. It is what occurs when our minds join with our brothers' and sisters' to experience wholeness. When we join in healing, we release our feelings of guilt and sin and replace them with joy and peace.

JUDGMENT — Judgment is our distorted opinion. It is our ego's mistaken belief that we have all of the facts necessary to evaluate and discern. When we judge others we are really judging ourselves.

LIGHT (SPIRITUAL LIGHT) — Light is anything that brings peace, love, joy, healing, and deeper spirituality. It is the Divine Presence in each of us.

MIRACLE — A miracle is a shift in perception.

It is the natural state of things when the flow of life is unobstructed. Miracles occur when, through the help of Spirit, we offer forgiveness and love instead of attack to a sister or brother. Miracles create healing, which releases us from guilt, fear, and anger. Miracles are not sized.

PEACE — Peace is a sense of well-being and calmness that allows light to flow through us, and allows miracles to be recognized more easily. It occurs when we are in the present moment and are not living in the past or future. Peace is our ultimate goal. We acquire it through healing (by forgiving and loving).

PERCEPTION — Perception is our interpretation of the world we live in. It is distorted by ego and is always changing because it is based on the ego's judgments (see SHIFT IN PERCEPTION).

PROJECTION — Projection is the process by which we get rid of our guilt, fear and anger by thrusting them onto someone or something else. "What we see outside ourselves is a reflection of what we see inside."

SHIFT IN PERCEPTION — A shift in perception is when we choose to see differently. Instead of listening to our ego (which brings up fear and guilt), we listen to Holy Spirit and extend the Love of God, which brings us peace. A *shift in perception* is a *miracle.*

SCARCITY — Scarcity is the belief that there is something lacking in me which forms the belief that there is also material lack in the world. (e.g. "I am not enough," and "There is not enough.")

SPIRIT — Spirit is often referred to as Holy Spirit. Spirit speaks to us in the language of love, truth, joy, and faith; it is our oneness with God. When we follow Spirit's guidance, peace, abundance, and growth are the results.

STORY — A story always talks about history— about the *past*, never the *present* moment. Often, ego will add drama and exaggeration to a story for more effect. When a story is used to preface a miracle, it brings turmoil to both the speaker and the listener.

VIGILANT FOR THE LIGHT — To be "vigilant

for the light" means that we constantly monitor our thoughts and what we see, hear, and say. Remember that we are not here to monitor others. We are here to be vigilant for the light in *ourselves* and our *interactions* with others. Vigilance requires that we carefully choose thoughts, conversations, activities, and relationships that will keep us in the light.

MIRACLE
JOURNAL

THESE PAGES HAVE BEEN PROVIDED FOR YOU TO RECORD YOUR PERSONAL MIRACLES

LESSON 1
I Watch What I Say

LESSON 2
I Notice What I Hear

LESSON 3
I Am Aware of What I See

LESSON 4
I Do Not Know the Real Meaning of What I See

LESSON 5
I Am Willing to See the Light

LESSON 6
I Am Vigilant for the Light

LESSON 7
I Am Very Prosperous

LESSON 8
Everyone Wishes to Contribute to Me

LESSON 9
I Deserve Prosperity

LESSON 10
I Am Open to Receive All of God's Gifts

LESSON 11
I Give As I Receive

LESSON 12
I Release All Fear

LESSON 13
I Open My Mind to Peace

LESSON 14
I Recognize My Own Best Interest

LESSON 15
I Am Patient

LESSON 16
I Pause Before I React

LESSON 17
I Am Open to Receive Miracles

LESSON 18
I Choose Only Peace

I Am a Loving and Lovable Child of God

LESSON 20
Only Love Exists; Fear Is an Illusion

LESSON 21
God Loves Me Unconditionally

LESSON 22
God Loves Me More Than I Love Myself

LESSON 23
I Trust God

LESSON 24
God Is Great and So Am I

LESSON 25
I Let Go and Let God

LESSON 26
I Am Blessed As a Child of God

LESSON 27
Today Belongs to God; It Is My Gift to Him

LESSON 28
I See Only God in All of My Affairs

LESSON 29
Thank You, God

LESSON 30
I Hear God's Voice All Day

EPILOGUE

This is not an end to this experience, but rather the beginning of your growth. Be open to the possibilities and remember:

WHO YOU REALLY ARE HAS NOTHING TO DO WITH WHAT YOU THINK OF YOURSELF

... BUT ...

EVERYTHING THAT HAPPENS OUTSIDE OF YOU IS A DIRECT RESULT OF WHAT YOU THINK OF YOURSELF.

ABOUT THE AUTHOR

Before practicing the principles contained in this book, Bijan had what most of us would refer to as a "fairly normal life" with the usual illnesses, failed relationships, and effortful income. Since using these principles, however, his life has been transformed. Excellent health, perfect relationships, and effortless prosperity are now the reality that Bijan enjoys. His prosperity consciousness and the directions from his guides have compelled him to share these simple lessons in the hope that others will receive as many miracles in their lives as he has.